LADY SECRETS

RODALE.
New York

LADY SECRETS

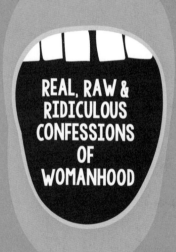

REAL, RAW &
RIDICULOUS
CONFESSIONS
OF
WOMANHOOD

Keltie Knight, Becca Tobin & Jac Vanek

Published in the United States by Rodale Books, an imprint of Random House,
a division of Penguin Random House LLC, New York.
RodaleBooks.com
RandomHouseBooks.com

RODALE and the Plant colophon are registered trademarks of
Penguin Random House LLC.

Library of Congress Cataloging-in-Publication Data is available upon request.

ISBN 978-0-593-23633-8
Ebook ISBN 978-0-593-23634-5

Printed in the United States of America

Cover design and illustrations: Jac Vanek
Author photograph: Claire Leahy
Interior illustrations: Wesley Bird

10 9 8 7 6 5 4 3 2 1

First Edition

CONTENTS

INTRODUCTION
A LADY NEVER TELLS

xi

PART ONE
FORGIVE ME, LADIES, FOR I HAVE SINNED: MORTIFYING CONFESSIONS WE NEED TO SET FREE

Jac: Poopnique	5
Keltie: My Final Rose	8
Becca: The B-Lister	14
Keltie: The Pee Was Me	17
Jac: Orgasm Oracle	22
Becca: The Unicorn	27
Keltie: The Real Walking Dead	30

LADYGANG CONFESSIONS

Sock It Poo Ya!	36
RIP Turbo	38
You Can't Catch a New Dog with Old Tricks	40
What Happens in Vegas Gets Stashed in the Sand	41
The Thera-*pissed*	42
National Fuckin' (Around) League	44
The Scholar-*shit*	44
Seven-Year Sitch	46
Hamslaughter	46

The Climb-ax 49
Snapped Chat 49
I Snooze, You Lose 51
The Sister Shocker 53
Not So Over Easy 54
Snitch Sitch 54
'Cuz I Love Him 56
The Batteries Are Dead 56
Liar's License 58
Brother Fucker 59
Celwyddog, Celwyddog! 61
Petty Cashing In 62

PART TWO

WELL, THIS IS AWKWARD: CRINGY CONFESSIONS THAT MAKE US WANT TO DISAPPEAR FOREVER

Jac: $4,000 Laxative 70
Keltie: The Oscar for the Shadiest Bitch
   Goes to . . . Me! 75
Becca: My Influencer Life 82
Jac: Wander-*bust* 84
Keltie: Au Revoir, Clooney! 91
Becca: Sunny-Side Up with a Side of Mortification 96

LADYGANG CONFESSIONS

A Tall Tail 98
This Date Sucks 99
Shitty Kitty 101
Vagina Flytrap 102
UR-ine Trouble 103
SEX-mergency 106
Pee-gasm 107
Hot Girl Bummer 108
What Would Gwyneth Do? 109

Going for Gold 112
What's the Buzz? 112
A Prime Mistake 115
Jail Mail 116
I'm So Wet Right Now 118

PART THREE
LIFE IS TOUGH, BUT SO ARE YOU: VULNERABLE CONFESSIONS THAT ARE DIFFICULT TO SHARE

Jac: Self-Love Is a Scam 127
Becca: Baby Blues 131
Keltie: My Hollywood Heartbreak 135
Becca: A Day to Remember 139
Keltie: Fucking Forties 145

LADYGANG CONFESSIONS

Therap-*me* 150
Daddy Issues 150
Friendless 151
One in Five Adults 152
Three-Year Nightmare 154
Addickted 155
I Hate Being a Mom 156
Postpartum Depression 156
A Monster 160

PART FOUR
GRABBING LIFE BY THE OVARIES: UNAPOLOGETIC CONFESSIONS THAT DESERVE A GOLD MEDAL

Jac: Scientology Cowboy 167
Becca: Built Ford Tough 175
Keltie: Julia Roberts Hates Me 179

Becca: The Maid of Dishonor 188
Jac: Josh Squared 190
Keltie: Murder on the Orient Express 198
Jac: Death by Penis 205

LADYGANG CONFESSIONS

Nip Sip 212
Nature's Lube 213
Gastric Lie-*pass* 214
What's My Age Again? 217
Someone Call Nev! 217
Triple Scoop 218
He Ate the Bait 220
No Regrets 221
Learning the Breaststroke 221
A Unique Arrangement 224
Childless Wonder 226
100% That Snitch 226
Shag 'n' Brag 227
Doc and Dash 230
Supercalifragilisticexpiali-felon 232
Revenge Is a Dish Best Served BBQ'd 233
There Is No "I" in Theft 235
You's a Hoe-gie 238
Charles in Charge 240

CONCLUSION
A LADY ALWAYS TELLS 243

ACKNOWLEDGMENTS 249

LADY SECRETS

A LADY NEVER TELLS

Every Lady has a secret. An experience or an encounter so disgraceful, so embarrassing, so shameful, or so *fucked up* that we wouldn't dare tell a single soul. Well, until now.

The truth is, we all do some disgusting, scandalous, heartbreaking, or generally ill-advised things when no one is watching. The humiliation of our darkest behaviors, the hilarity of our grossest moments, the torment of our most raw memories—these all become our *secrets*. Secrets we hold deep inside and refuse to even tell our closest friends, families, lovers, or doctors. But as they say: The truth will set you free.

Over the years, the three of us have released many of our own mortifying stories into the universe on the *LadyGang* podcast and in our first book, *Act Like a Lady*. And with every secret we shed, we felt like we were doing a small service to ourselves and ladyhood in general. By sharing the not-so-pretty truths of our lives, we felt like we were dropping the mask of perfection society forces upon us—pulling back the curtain and leveling the playing field for ladies everywhere and saying, "Enough is enough!"

For some insane reason, society has imposed on women a false standard in which it feels shameful to show the struggles of figuring out womanhood, and because of this, we always make ourselves appear more pulled together, smart, and stylish than we actually are. On top of that, we are all competing in the "Lady Olympics," and we worry that admitting that we acted selfishly, broke the rules, or fucked our brother-in-law in Cuba might take us down a notch in the eyes of all of the judgmental pricks out there. Women are *not* allowed to be messy. We are supposed to be polished and obedient and accommodating, right? We've become so damn afraid of drawing outside of the lines that we keep even the most innocuous secrets deep in our personal vaults.

Our goal with this book is to embrace the power of our genuine selves by owning our *un*ladylike truth. Men get to brag to their friends about their inappropriate behaviors—they wear their sinful stories like a badge of honor, and society in general tends to shrug it off or enable their reckless behavior. (Boys will be boys, right?) But women? We carry around a lot more shame about our behaviors than men do and tend to hide our secrets out of fear of being labeled imperfect. Because society expects us, as women, to *do it all*. We're supposed to have a career, change the diapers, clean the kitchen, and impress others with a smile on our face and our tits up to our shoulders. God forbid we lose something up our vaginas and have to go to the emergency room! The double standard for the expected behaviors for men and women is unfair and straight-up misogynistic, and, quite frankly, we're fuckin' sick of it.

Don't you feel this sense of deep *relief* when you hear another lady share some juicy, behind-the-scenes blooper from her life? We know *we* do. It makes us feel less alone, less ashamed, and more human. And we wanted to give that priceless gift to our LadyGang community and fellow ladies around the world.

So we created Lady Secrets.

Not only do we reveal many of our deepest, darkest secrets in this book, but we have also gone above and beyond. Even though our Gang is a collective of the most wonderful, wise, incredible women, we knew that each of you bitches was hiding *something*—just like us! So, we launched a submission website and hotline, 1-844-SXY-LADY, which gives others the opportunity to join in shedding the shame and embrace the power of revealing their truths. The secrets immediately started flooding in. Lady Secrets became a space for our ladies to expose their dustiest skeletons and free themselves from the guilt that weighed them down. And the result? A dynamic collection of essays, short stories, unsolicited advice, and lessons learned the hard way. We're exploring universal truths that will make you shudder: white lies turned lifelong cons, weird things our bodies do, messy sex lives, and juicy celebrity encounters, while also shining a light on the gut-wrenching secrets about motherhood, relationships, death, revenge, and depression.

This is our collective truth, and we hope it inspires you to embrace yours as well. Lady life is exciting and beautiful and scary and rewarding and grueling and sketchy and agonizing and smelly. And we're here to share it all: the good, the bad, and the diarrhea. So, to every Lady who submitted a hilariously disturbing tale or left us a ridiculous voicemail, we congratulate you on your courage. From getting a fly stuck up your vagina to straight-up hating being a mother, your secrets made us laugh, cry, and cringe deep in our souls.

A note: Submissions to the book have been edited for clarity and length. (If you pooped in a barbecue grill for revenge and submitted your story, but it doesn't sound exactly the same, trust us, it's your poop. Thanks for understanding!)

We hope *Lady Secrets* leaves you feeling a little less worried about your awkward memories, a little less ashamed of your *un*ladylike habits, and a little less alone. Because, we think we can all agree, stumbling through womanhood is a lot easier when you know everyone else is stumbling alongside you.

PART ONE

FORGIVE ME, LADIES, FOR I HAVE SINNED

Mortifying Confessions We Need to Set Free

Maybe it's a little white lie that's spiraled out of control. Maybe you're still holding on to guilt about something you did as a child. Maybe you truly did something *super* fucked up, and you never admitted it to anyone in real life. Whatever it is, we are all holding on to *something*—either for good reason or not—that we simply need to get off our chests. This section is just for that.

As humans, we all tend to want the outside world to see us as having our life together. Many of us still present our "highlight reel," even to our closest friends. Living in the digital age, where everything is documented, is terrifying. What if we share a private story via text and someone screenshots it and blasts it all over social media? What if a best friend becomes an ex–best friend, and they have years of ammo that illustrates why you might be a terrible or disgusting person? Sharing our secrets with others is scary; we understand.

But carrying the crushing weight of these types of secrets makes us feel like hot garbage—so why do we do it? Our not-scientific-at-all research leads us to believe that as a baseline, women are *used* to feeling like hot garbage. Our boobs are sore, our cramps are debilitating, we have extreme mood swings, and we literally expel blood out of our vaginas for one week every month. On top of that, we pluck hairs, laser our hoo-has, and wear terrible high heels that make our feet bleed, underwire bras that dig into our rib cages, and itchy thongs that ride up our butts, because *beauty is pain.* Despite all that, we keep conquering our lives like it's no big deal. So adding the shame of our secrets to our physical and emotional backpack of life honestly feels like a walk in the park.

Admitting that we messed up, even if it's a hilarious story

that would be the highlight of any dinner party, somehow always feels like a failure. And that's because we are fed a diet of *women having it all.** There is so much perfection being beamed into our brains every single day, and we are groomed to be shiny little fembots programmed to never falter or fall.

But whether it's Facetuning your pictures on Bumble, fibbing about the year you were born to stay on your parents' health insurance, or creating an entire fabricated identity for the fun of it, everyone out there is lying about *something you just want to get off your chest.*

Our main takeaway for Part One? STOP LETTING YOUR SECRETS WEIGH YOU DOWN. We're not saying you need to shout them from the rooftops (God, please don't). But as we've established, women are not perfect—including you! So if you feel like you're shoving things down in the name of keeping up appearances, we have an assignment for you: Read this section, put your own shit into context, and then fess up to something small with a friend you trust. All of the women around you have their own humiliating secrets, and admitting that you are not perfect is the first step to setting your spirit free.

JAC: POOPNIQUE

This is something I truly have never told a soul before now. Not my best friend, not my partner, not my doctor . . . no one. I was going to take this one to the grave, but I guess that's the point of our book, right? Sharing our deepest and darkest in hopes that someone out there in this big bad world relates. So, here it goes:

I poop with my feet on the toilet. Not like . . . my feet touching the toilet. I poop with the bottoms of my soles on the toilet seat. Tucked in, right against my butt. Fetal position. Perched up there like a goddamn gargoyle.

I'm sure you're reading this thinking . . . *what . . . how . . . why?????* Well, you see, I had been using a Squatty Potty to aid in my bowel movements for as long as I can remember. If you're unfamiliar with this overpriced piece of genius, the Squatty Potty is essentially a little twelve-inch step you hoist your feet up on while you're sitting to go poop. Something about the angle of your hips helps the poop make its way out of your butthole effortlessly. Hell, why am I trying to explain this like I'm some poop expert?! Let's go straight to the source. Per the Squatty Potty website:

> Your body relies on a bend in the colon (where your poop lives) and the anus (where your poop says hi) to keep everything stored until showtime. The posture of the western toilet causes a kink in this tunnel, which leads to major blockage. Squatty Potty undoes this kink so you can do business the way you were meant to.

(By the way, whoever writes the copy for Squatty Potty is my fucking soulmate. Anyway!)

So essentially what I'm getting from that blurb is that when we were cavemen, we didn't have these uber-comfortable porcelain thrones (some with heated seats and lots of fun buttons and water that shoots up your butthole!) to do our business on. We just had to squat on the ground and shit in a little pile and *not* wipe off our dingleberries and just go on with our lives hunting and gathering (OH MY GOD?!). I guess the evolution of human anatomy—when it comes to pooping—hasn't caught up to the invention of the toilet, and that little tweakment in the hip angle makes all the difference!

So anyway, yes, I used a Squatty Potty. And it worked! Coming from someone with constant constipation, it truly was a godsend . . . until a few years ago, when my Squatty Potty got lost in a move to a new apartment. I woke up the first morning at my brand-new little home, drank my morning coffee, and it was time to do my business. I got to the toilet, went to pull out my Squatty Potty, and . . . it wasn't there. And I legit *lost my mind.* Nooooooooo! How would I poop???? I needed that glorious little ledge. It was my crutch! I tried to stack a few books up at the foot of the toilet, but the angle wasn't right. Then I tried to just hold up my legs and hover my feet off the ground, but I was *far* too out of shape to hold that for more than ten seconds. And then, in the most meaningful lightbulb moment of my life, I slowly lifted up my feet and placed them on the toilet. And it was like Elon Musk's hyperloop train speeding through a tunnel at 760 mph! IT WAS THE BEST POOP OF MY LIFE. After that fateful day, I've never once pooped *without* my knees tucked into my chest.

So, the moral of the story? Save yourself $39 and tuck those tootsies right on up on the toilet seat like you're back in the womb! *But* . . . if someone at Squatty Potty is reading this, let's collaborate on the Squatty Potty Extreme™.

KELTIE: MY FINAL ROSE

After living in New York for a decade and spending almost two entire years on the road as a professional touring dancer, I decided to get some sunshine and try my luck in Los Angeles. One of my best friends lived there, so I snagged an apartment up the street from her and then spent the next month running around in a black fishnet catsuit trying *unsuccessfully* to book a job. For example, I spent two full days of my life auditioning for Christina Aguilera, only to have her creative team hire just the dancers that she had worked with previously. Essentially, they did us all DIRRRRTTTYYYYY . . . what a big waste of time.

In the middle of trying very hard to be a backup dancer, I was not trying *at all* to be a television host. But, to be honest, when you are desperate for ways to pay rent, you'll apply for every job you are qualified for, and almost all of the ones you are wrong for, too. (I once went to an audition for women who played bass guitar. Spoiler alert: I don't play bass guitar.) Being a TV host had never occurred to me; I didn't even own a television. Everyone that's known me since 2000 when I moved to New York City has learned that I read books and put my extra money in an emergency fund. I would never waste any amount of money buying something as stupid as a TV. By the time this book comes out I will have won three Emmy Awards for appearing, and also make a living appearing, on TV . . . but I digress.

During this time in my life, I had started a blog that had gained a bit of a following. Eventually, that rolled into getting a part-time job as a staff writer with a company called Buzznet, but only under the premise of my own "blog." Sometimes, a weird opportunity to make a blog video would come along; this was way before streaming services, TikTok, Instagram reels, or any video at all really existed on the internet; even YouTube was brand new. For fun, I had been dabbling in the medium, editing videos of my Rockette shenanigans between shows of the Radio City *Christmas Spectacular.* My series, "End Girl, Stage Right," had a whopping total of about 140 views. I was obviously destined for stardom.

Somehow through a friend, I landed a meeting with one of the top hosting agents in Hollywood. I'm actually not sure if this person was a top hosting agent, but it was sold to me as a star-making event, and so I went. When I got there, the agent took one look at me and my résumé, which was filled primarily with backup dancing for superstars and/or high kicking for Santa Claus, and said, "Well, Keltie, if you want to be a host, you should just go on *The Bachelor.*" I went home that night, found the website to apply, and immediately put in my application. Had I ever seen *The Bachelor?* It's unclear. All I knew was that it involved falling in love and wearing pretty dresses . . . and I vaguely remembered that back in high school I may have watched Tristan and Ryan get married and then read in some "magazine" in the grocery store checkout line that they got paid $1 million to say "I do" on TV. I also have some memory of seeing the contestants on the covers of *Us Weekly* on my daily walks around the corner from my shitty LA apartment to the 76 gas station to buy my meal of the day: one large fountain Diet Coke and a sleeve of vanilla wafers. I did not know what the hell I was getting myself into, but it seemed like the advice the "top agent" had given me was correct. If I wanted to be a television host or be famous, I simply needed to get on *The Bachelor*. Also, at the time, I was a shell of a human being, having recently been heartbroken from a pretty public breakup (fine, it had been a year, but whatever). I had unsuccessfully tried online dating while on tour, and I was lonely and desperate. And, I may have written that, verbatim, on my application.

When I received the email that the show wanted me to come down to their Santa Monica offices to audition, I was stoked! I felt like I was crushing Top Agent's plan! No more standing in line for hours a day in booty shorts and bras for low-paying dance jobs for me! Instead I was on my way to becoming America's Canadian Sweetheart (which wasn't too lofty a dream since my childhood friend Kaitlyn Bristowe went on to do precisely that many years later).

I arrived for my audition desperately codependent and heart-breakingly single in a blue-and-white-striped V-neck T-shirt. After twenty minutes of talking about myself, they thanked me, and I was on my merry little way. I never really thought about it again and instead focused on my new shimmer-tight-less career as a television host (who did not own a television). I signed up for a "How to Be a Host" class with Suzanne Sena, and a few months later, after a few rounds of auditions (and, shockingly, with almost no experience), I booked a pretty big job as a music host for a big music company. Lack of experience be damned. It did make sense in a way. I mean, I had been a backup dancer for many musicians, I had had sex with many musicians, and I was hoping to have more sex with even more musicians in my future. It really was the perfect job for me.

Little did I know how much this gig would alter the course of my life. While I don't exactly remember the introduction, I met (spoiler: my future husband) Chris Knight while working this job. Chris and I just instantly clicked, and I remember thinking on our first, second, and third dates, *Wow, this guy is really great, and he really seems to like me!*, which was super shocking, because I really wasn't used to anyone thinking I was lust-worthy at this point in my life. I was an absolute pathetic husk of a human being at that moment, and it all seemed way too easy. I was super scared waiting for the other shoe to drop. Sure, I'd let him come help me load up some Craigslist furniture into my Honda CR-V, but I wasn't giving him any of my true heart!

At the same time Chris and I were doing this weird courting dance (and so many months after my audition for *The Bachelor* that I had forgotten that I had ever had the meeting), I got the email inviting me to the Bachelor Mansion to be a part of the show! So, I did what any ordinary twenty-something who had started dating someone that they thought had potential but had no faith in real love would do: I sat Chris Knight down at the 101 Café, ordered breakfast, and proceeded to tell him that I could *not* be his girlfriend because I was going to be on *The Bachelor*.

He cried. It was awful. At that time in my life, I was so career-driven that I had given up on ever finding "the one." I'd been let down by every single man I'd ever trusted. Even though things seemed to be going well with Chris, in my head I was thinking, *Yeah, I mean I like you, but you're probably going to turn into a dick in two months.* And, there was no way I was going to miss my opportunity to check the box on what Top Agent told me was the most-important-thing-to-do in order to become a television host. So, bye, CK.

Here's the lady secret: I have lied about this timeline to almost everyone in my life for the last eleven-plus years. I share with you now one striking detail that only Chris Knight and I know about. Not only did I decide I would *not* be Chris Knight's girlfriend and ditch him to go on *The Bachelor,* but I also made this lovely man take me shopping—for an entire Saturday—for the perfect (under $50) gown to wear for my impending victory-slash-proposal on the finale of a show I had never seen before.

That is so twisted and dark that I'm going to need you to go back, reread the previous paragraph, and then continue on this journey. Also, Chris Knight, you are the love of my life, *but you should have dropped me like a hot cake, baby.*

Next, I took my Chris Knight–approved gown, two months of clothing, some terrible hair extensions, my one-shouldered mini dresses, and my lucky feather earring, and moved into a hotel by the airport to begin my journey to Love.

When you go on *The Bachelor,* they take away your phone, books, and passport, and then they make the TVs play the same three movies nonstop. They lock you in a hotel room for a few days and make you stir-crazy so when the first night begins, you are a bundle of nerves, emotions, and energy! I have to be honest, I am very proud of my limo entrance. I performed a sensual développé into a high kick while wearing an Alice and Olivia mini sheath and sky-high Louboutins. *Did someone say front-runner?* Buuuuuuuut, that's really where the fun of *The Bachelor* ended for me. I specifically remember walking up to Brad

Womack's face, which was plastered with heavy television makeup, to introduce myself and feeling immediate apprehension. Sure, this man looked like a living Ken doll, but he wasn't MY Chris, my gentle giant with kind little eyes and rock-and-roll hair. My heart sank; I knew I had made a huge mistake.

The good news is that Brad had horrible taste in women (just kidding) and didn't like me either. My stay on *The Bachelor* was so short, most people don't even know I was on the show. Here's the rundown: I made it past the first rose ceremony, went on a group date wearing a neck brace and two arm casts, spent one day by the pool at the Bachelor Mansion, and saw Ashley Spivey naked in the shower precisely one time; then I was promptly rejected and dejected by Brad Womack.

My exit interview, which you can still watch online, is hysterical. I'm wearing a one-shoulder purple mini dress, my lucky feather earring, and janky hair extensions topped with a metal chain-link headpiece. I am crying about love like I am goddamn Meryl Streep. The performance is incredible. How on earth anyone (especially within the first two episodes) can work themselves into this level of hysteria is amazing, since at this point, I had spent ninety seconds total with the man. But, the truth is, the tears were real. I wasn't crying over Brad Womack or about being ejected from a competition I knew almost nothing about. I was sad that I "lost," because I hate losing. I was sad about being publicly humiliated in a challenge where I was told to dress and act like a "butch queen" (which, in the year that we are currently in, would never fucking fly). I was crying because that's what I do, whether I am getting rejected on the dance floor for a Broadway show or from a guy I didn't even know. Worst of all, I was grieving my chance to fall in love with Chris Knight and embarrassed I had put my career and selfish ways ahead of building a relationship with a fucking good human. Rejection sucks. Rejection is even worse when you're wearing a chain-link headband and a one-shoulder sequin mini on national television. Wow, I feel so free! I'm happy to report that the first thing I did when *The Bachelor* producers gave me my phone back was call Chris Knight and ask him (through my tears), "Will you be my boyfriend?" His answer? "Oh, hell yeah!" And we lived happily ever after. Chris and I even celebrated our first Halloween together with a Bachelor-themed couples costume, complete with red roses, him in a tux, and me in my $50 yellow finale gown that he had picked out for me that fateful day so many months before.

BECCA: THE B-LISTER

The year was 2012 and I had just moved to Los Angeles to start working on *Glee*. For the first couple months in LA, my life felt a little surreal. There I'd be, sitting next to Kate Hudson in the makeup trailer or sharing pizza on set with Gwyneth or zooming around the famed Paramount lot in a golf cart. Let's not forget the half-naked magazine photoshoots or the paparazzi waiting outside of restaurants for me . . . it was insane. My New York friends joked it was inevitable that I would turn into the quintessential narcissistic Hollywood scumbag, but I knew I'd be okay; I always prided myself on not giving a shit about celebrities or fame. Even during my Broadway years, when celebrities would come backstage to say hi or take pics with the cast, I was always the super chill one. I knew how to handle myself. And, as far as my taste in men went, I was more a cleat chaser than a star fucker, so I pretty much felt immune to the industry bullshit. With that all said . . . this secret feels pretty brutal to share.

After a couple months in LA, I was invited to one of the many lame Hollywood events on the rooftop of some hotel on Sunset Boulevard. (For anyone unfamiliar with Los Angeles, the location was super cliché and incredibly cringeworthy.) I took a girlfriend with me as my plus-one (instead of my boyfriend at the time) because, while I genuinely loved my boyfriend and I'm not a fame whore, I'm also not a complete fucking idiot. You don't land on the scene in LA at twenty-six years old and start bringing your boyfriend with you to industry events. I was savvy enough to know that that was *not* the vibe, nor was it a good career move. We planned to just "pop by" the event for a quick see-and-be-seen moment and would meet up with our boyfriends afterward for dinner.

Upon arrival, we mingled, drank champagne, and soon found ourselves chatting it up with a familiar B-list gentleman who—to my surprise—seemed to be putting some sexy vibes in my direction. Within two months of being in LA I had quite the rude awakening: In terms of looks, I was about a "4" in Hollywood. The only men who hit on me at these Hollywood parties were the man-boys at the valet or the crusty old "manager" types who were there accompanying their (even less successful than me) actor clients. This B-lister flirting with me had been linked to famous models and gorgeous actresses! I couldn't help but be flattered that he was mildly interested in making eyes at me.

We had been bantering it up for a while with the B-list hottie when our phones started blowing up. We were fifteen minutes late for our dinner reservation, and our significant others were getting testy. It was time to get the fuck out of there. I mustered the strength to tell the cutie that it was lovely chatting, but we had to head out.

B-LISTER: What?! Absolutely not. Where are you going?

LOSER BECCA: We have a dinner that we are already late for. (I failed to mention it was with our boyfriends because I was a weak, weak woman.)

B-LISTER: Too bad. Call and cancel. You're coming with me to Beacher's Madhouse.

For those of you who don't know LA, Beacher's Madhouse is where you go to make bad decisions. It's pretty much LA's craziest nightclub, featuring entertainers of all kinds (use your imagination) and where the cocaine *allegedly* flows like the salmon of Capistrano.

Feeling the pressure and excitement, my girlfriend and I retreated to the bathroom to devise our game plan. Neither of us wanted the fun to end, but we needed to come up with something. (Key plot point: This friend is the kind of gal who lives by the mantra, "We only get one trip here on earth, so have fun and feel hot!" At that moment, she was quite possibly the best/worst person to have advising me.) We laid it on thick and decided to tell our boyfriends that—for our friendship—we *really needed* a girls night, and we were going to stay a little longer.

I have *no idea* why I didn't get dumped at that moment, but it worked! Before you could say "triflin' hoe," we were off to Beacher's Madhouse. I promised myself I wouldn't make any bad decisions; I was just going to flirt a little bit. (I can feel you judging me, but my ego needed this after the endless barrage of tweets I had endured comparing my new *Glee* character to a sad housewife in a cheerleading costume.)

I was a few lukewarm cranberry vodka cocktails in when the night started to make that notorious transition from kinda fun to slightly hazy . . . and maybe even a touch creepy. The next thing I knew, I was getting a weak-ass shoulder massage from the B-lister in our private banquette. I couldn't help but wonder how many women this move actually worked on. I shot my girlfriend a look, and she must have received my subliminal message because, within four minutes, we said some awkwardly hasty good-byes and were in a cab. Sure, I may have been an insecure loser, but I wasn't ready to cheat on my boyfriend.

I still see this B-lister all over the place and even once ran into him. He proceeded to introduce himself to me *as if we had never met and shared this worthless evening.* So glad I made such a strong impression!

KELTIE: THE PEE WAS ME

Generally, there are two kinds of family trees. There are the massive families, with seven children on each side and cousins galore, and there are the people like me with tiny families, so small that my mom and dad made everyone an "honorary" grandpa, grandma, or auntie to cover the fact that we didn't have enough family to go around. I won't bore you with the details, but between the French Canadians, the Scottish immigrants, the First Nation fam, the adoptions, and the deaths, my family tree is more like a giant shrub growing wild in the front yard. Let's just say I called *a lot* of people Grandma.

This story is about one of my favorite fake grandmas, "Grandma Hays." (Hilariously, while recounting this story, I am just realizing that I called fake grandma "Grandma Hays," but called her husband, John, "*Uncle* John." This makes absolutely no sense, and at the same time makes perfect sense with my fucked-up family.) Grandma Hays wasn't my real grandma; she was one of my mom's best friend's moms. She took my mom under her wing when my biological grandmother passed away while my mom was in college.

Grandma Hays was a tough cookie; she insisted on perfect manners. You had to be polite and do your chores. She certainly did not like a young lady who, *God forbid*, wore a hairstyle with bangs. She was a no-bullshit kind of woman, and I loved her because she would always make me my favorite sandwich (sugar-and-cinnamon toast) and because she loved my two favorite things: First, she loved to craft and taught me how to knit and crochet. Second, Grandma Hays was a fierce-ass tap-dancing queen. Even into her nineties, she'd put on her black tights and bodysuit each week to dance with her troupe, "the Crockettes" (like the Radio City Rockettes, but old . . . and crockety?). Every time we were together, she would ask me how my tap dancing was going. She never got to see me on the Radio City stage, but, to be honest, I'm happy she died before I became the infamous Rockette who was called out in front of the entire company multiple times for faking her "left single wings" in the twelve-minute tap extravaganza for the "Twelve Days of Christmas."

My tap skills were somewhat subpar, and if she had not already died, I would have killed her with my inferior tap skills on the big stage while simultaneously ruining Christmas.

Growing up, I spent a lot of time at her off-the-grid lake cabin on Cooking Lake in Alberta, Canada. Cooking Lake's name comes from its native Cree-Indian name. And while it seemed like the Four Seasons Maui to me, looking back, it was far from it. Cooking Lake's only Google review states, "Okay, this place is hard to find, and when you see it, disappointing. Save your gas money and time, there's no beach, the people in the area are very rude, and overall it isn't worth the two hours or more it will take to find this place." On Reddit, it's described as a "shallow slough" and at its deepest is "five feet." You couldn't even swim in the lake. There were so many bugs and leeches that my mom used to say, "You'll get the itch." The actual cabin had a screen door that used to bang open and closed. It must've had electricity, although I can't remember the lights ever being on, and there were no signs of technology. We barbecued, drank lukewarm sodas out of a useless fridge, and washed all the dishes by hand in a giant sink of dirty water. To kid-me, it was heaven!

Every once in a while, Grandma Hays would "treat" the kids to an overnight sleepover. We would hang out, play Uno, talk about boys and acne and try out shimmery lipsticks that we had to hide from our dads. It was awesome because we had the absolute freedom to do pretty much whatever we wanted. There was only one downside to sleepovers at Grandma Hays's house: We had to use the outhouse on the property. And yes, while Grandma Hays was known in the community for having the best-smelling outhouse ever (whatever that means), I was terrified of outhouses. If you haven't had the pleasure of using one, let me explain. There are so many decisions to make when you go in: Do you breathe? Do you breathe through your nose? While you squat, do you look outward toward the spiders hiding in the wooden corners, or do you look down at your feet where the creepy crawly multi-legged bugs crawl across your toes? Do you look down the hole? (Hot tip: WHATEVER YOU DO, DO NOT LOOK DOWN THE HOLE.) I would get in and out as quickly as possible.

The middle of the night pees were a different story. The yard and outhouse were pitch black, so Grandma Hays left a tiny white-and-black-speckled bedpan underneath the bed in the guestroom where we slept. It was expected that if you used it during the night that you could leave the pee there until morning, under the bed. But, as soon as you woke up in the morning, Grandma's number one rule was that it was your job to take the bedpan, empty it, clean it out, and put it back. No one else was responsible for your piss. I was about eight or nine years old during this time and at a stage where I was embarrassed about any and all bodily functions. (LadyGang fans know I've come a long way, right?) Naturally, I just pretended that I *never* had to pee or poop. I would blush uncomfortably when Grandma reminded us about the rule with the bedpan; I was so embarrassed that we even had to talk about going to the bathroom in front of our grandma.

One night in late August, a storm was brewing up over Cooking Lake. My friend Cath (an actual grandkid) and I were curled up together in the guest room at Grandma's cabin, under a handmade quilt. We fell asleep talking about boys, thinking about boys, and figuring out how we could get boys to like us when we got back to school in September. In the middle of the night, I was awoken with the urge to pee. It was dark, and I squatted over that royal blue carpet, aimed as best I could, and peed directly into the bedpan. When I was done, I shoved it under the bed with my foot and went back to sleep.

In the morning, Cath and I got up, ate some breakfast, and, of course, were chatting it up about boys. The sun was shining, and we went out to play in the forest to spend another fabulous day at Cooking Lake. Suddenly we heard Grandma Hays calling us into the cabin. She was livid. She looked at Cath and me. She held the bedpan in her hands, tilted it toward our faces, and said sternly, "Whose pee is this?"

I lied. I said, "It's not mine," and I looked at my friend. Cath shot me a quizzical look but was firm in her denial, too. "It's not mine," she said definitively, which only made Grandma angrier. What I *should* have done was confess that I had been in such a deep sleep that I barely remembered peeing in the bedpan, reminded her that I was the kind of girl who didn't like to break the rules, so if I had remembered, even just a little bit, I obviously would have cleaned up after myself. But I was scared of getting in trouble, so I straight-up lied. I shook my head and swore on my life that it wasn't my pee.

My loyal friend, who knew that I was guilty, didn't rat me out, because we knew each other's deepest, darkest secrets about boys. Together we faced the wrath of Grandma and split the responsibility of cleaning out that bedpan. I have stayed true to that lie until this book.

I'm revealing my Lady Secret: the pee was me. I'm sorry that I lied. And, Cath, I'm sorry that I forced you to get in trouble for something you didn't do.

Grandma Hays, I'm sorry that I lied to you and that I never came clean before you passed away. I'm also sad to admit that my tap skills never improved over the years. I am sorry for my bad single left wings. I know you probably watched me from Heaven dancing with the Rockettes and felt proud until you saw me butcher that piece of technique, and then rolled your eyes every time the "Twelve Days of Christmas" started playing. I would genuinely do anything to go back to the simplicity of life with you at Cooking Lake, playing in the forest, and being cut off from a world of cell phones and pressure. It would be my great honor to clean my pee out of a bedpan or take a spin in the nicest outhouse in the west.

JAC: ORGASM ORACLE

What gets you off? Yeah, I'm asking you what makes you orgasm. Maybe it's watching porn or fantasizing about Chris Hemsworth or deeply connecting with your partner in the moment. Not me. Nope. Wanna know what gets me off? The texture of unfinished clay. Or a plastic beach ball. Or a blade of grass under a microscope. No, I'm not romanticizing these things like I'm about to make a TikTok montage with a sparkly filter and a clip of Olivia Rodrigo's "Drivers License" as the soundtrack. And, no, I'm absolutely not *sexually attracted* to these things (though I have seen people on Maury's *My Strange Addiction* who are . . . no hate), but it's what makes me orgasm. I know, this makes no sense. And I know I'm a fucking weirdo. But let me explain.

I have this thing called synesthesia, which is defined by Healthline.com as "a neurological condition in which information meant to stimulate one of your senses stimulates several of your senses." I know what you're thinking. *WTF Jac, explain this shit like I'm five.* For me, in its very simplest form, sometimes *I feel colors.* But probably not how you're thinking. I'm not walking through a rainbow-filled acid trip, and I'm definitely not living that Popsicle commercial from the nineties ("The colors, Duke, the colors!"). It's more that certain random things evoke an overwhelming sensation of specific colors in my being. And let me make it clear, I don't *see* colors, I literally *feel* them throughout my body. Yep, I feel colors in my head, shoulders, knees, and toes!

For some things, my synesthesia is vague. Here's some examples:

NUMBERS
Odd numbers are cool colors.
Even numbers are warm colors.

DIRECTIONS
Left is cool.
Right is warm.

DAYS OF THE WEEK
Monday, Wednesday, and Friday
   are warm.
Tuesday and Thursday are cool.
Saturday and Sunday have no color.

SCHOOL SUBJECTS
Math is green.
Science is blue.
History is orange.
English is red.

For other things, my synesthesia is more detailed. Instead of feeling generally warm or cool color sensations, I feel *very* distinct colors. Music gets me goooood, especially music that I listen to constantly. My fiancé's band, The Maine, released a record called *XOXO* that stimulates my synesthesia super big-time for every song. These are the colors I feel listening to each song:

"Sticky"—robin's-egg blue

"Lips"—fire-engine red

"Love in Real Time"—dark, dull gray

"High Forever"—deep, rich magenta

"April 7th"—muted turquoise

"If Your Light Goes Out"—dark, vibrant cerulean

"Pretender"—neon green

"Dirty, Pretty, Beautiful"—bright lemon

"Anxiety in Real Time"—steel blue

"Face Towards the Sun"—pastel tangerine

For those of you who aren't superfans of The Maine, I feel the following for a few of the classics:

"Lucy in the Sky with Diamonds"—bright purple

"I Want It That Way"—baby blue

"Bohemian Rhapsody"—dark black

"Semi-Charmed Life"—bright yellow

"Hit Me Baby One More Time"—bubblegum pink

"Smells Like Teen Spirit"—muted gray

"Don't Stop Believing"—cerulean blue

But nothing, and I mean *nothing* is more detailed than when I have an orgasm. My synesthesia doesn't kick in with all of my orgasms, it only happens under a very specific set of circumstances. It only starts during my *second* orgasm, when I use my Magic Wand to do my lady business. Which, side note . . . if you don't own a Magic Wand, get your ass on Amazon right now and SMASH that "Buy Now" button. I'm talking ten orgasms in a row. You can thank me later.

My orgasm synesthesia started super vague back in the day. In the beginning, when my orgasm would slowly start to build, faint shades of color would creep into focus in my mind. As the orgasm grew, so would the colors, until they *exploded* into this incredible, intense, and detailed heightened sensation throughout my entire body when the orgasm actually hit. What started as just feeling colors has evolved into feeling textures, temperatures, and sometimes full-on visual scenes when my orgasm hits. And now the only way to actually reach an orgasm when this starts happening is to hyperfocus on whatever pops into my brain and give in to the synesthesia. Every orgasm is different, and I've never seen the same vision twice. Bizarre, right?! I've started to compile an ongoing list of the random shit I feel when orgasming. Enjoy:

Calico cat fur

The bouncing silver balls from a 5 Gum commercial

Bright pink chewed bubblegum

Those green Styrofoam balls from Michaels

The Game of Thrones metallic logo letters

Macro view of a bumblebee

Tea-soaked parchment paper

A crinkled-up potato chip bag

Purple crushed velvet

Fire in the Backdraft ride at Universal Studios

A fake daisy flower

Warm soap bubbles in a kitchen sink

Cowhide rug

Reddish-brown sanding paper

The squishy plastic of a blown-up beach ball

The green, waxy leaf of a monstera plant

A blue, soft cotton Hawaiian shirt

The condensation on a cold water bottle

Coffee grounds

Sticky leather seats in a hot car

The cork from a wine bottle

Scratchy, unfinished cedarwood

The fabric on Yeezy sneakers

Periwinkle matte plastic

Black iPhone screen

Macro view of champagne bubbles

Hot, dusty concrete

Bright turquoise felt square

Streetlamps on a foggy night

Bright pink-and-orange sunset

Sugar in the Raw

An orange, itchy wool sweater

Damp cardboard

A bright redbrick wall

Fine white sand

Religious stained-glass window

Dense, bright green moss

Limestone

Macro view of the inside of a kiwi

Handful of uncooked rice

The scales on a crocodile

Watercolor flowers

Smashed-up avocado

Blue-and-white canvas umbrella

Tan exterior of a G-Wagon

A light gray, puffy down coat

Macro view of a bicycle wheel

A fireman's uniform

Christmas lights

Dr. Martens combat boot soles

A pile of leaves in the fall

Skin

Steaming-hot chicken noodle soup

The universe

So there you have it. When I started experiencing ⟨
synesthesia, I was pretty damn confused, and honestly a littl⟨
embarrassed. But the more I research it, the more fascinated
become. Plus, there's gotta be some other people out there who
envision a steel water bottle instead of Jason Momoa when they
get off, right??

Will my synesthesia continue to evolve? Probably. Am I some
oracle that can tell the future through my orgasms? Most likely.
I'll keep you updated if I unlock the key to time travel with my
Magic Wand and find myself in a wormhole one day!

BECCA: THE UNICORN

In my early twenties, I ran around NYC with the coolest and
most fun musical theater performers. I spent a ton of time with
this group for about a year of my life. We shared many de-
bauched nights out together, and they are still some of my favorite memories. All of the guys in this particular circle were gay (a
very normal statistic for a bunch of theater kids at that time).
Well, all but *one*. And, it's pretty common knowledge that a
straight guy in musical theater was the proverbial needle in
a haystack. Because of his rarity, he could look like Shrek, be a
total asshole, *and* have a micropenis but still get laid every night
of the week by some hot, beautiful dancer. However, this particular straight guy possessed none of those qualities . . . so he
was basically a unicorn.

For as long as I had known him, Straight Guy was linked to

iend—whom I had never met—and who was
y (for me) out of town. However, everyone in
w her raved about her and couldn't wait for
ıuse they "knew [we] would be best friends!"

l think, *Ummmm ya, if your best friend got
⸺ ⸺ every weekend and tried to bone your boyfriend while you
were out of town.* Yup, Becca at twenty years old = impulsive +
selfish. I didn't give a shit about this mystery woman! Plus, this
was before social media, so I couldn't even put a face with the
girlfriend's name!! How could I possibly care about a woman I
couldn't even Insta-stalk?! If the musical theater dating scene
was a sexless desert, then Straight Guy was my mirage, and I
took every opportunity to shamelessly flirt. To SG's credit—as
flirty as he ever was, and much to my disappointment—he *never
caved.* Which obviously made me even more aggressive with
each night out. (An actual shudder goes through my body now
when I think about my level of thirst.)

So . . . the months went by, and my failed attempts became
extremely humbling. I eventually just threw in the towel . . . *just
kidding*—his girlfriend finally returned home. The time had
come for me to finally meet the famous (dreaded) lover of my
straight-man crush. Much to my chagrin, she was just as beautiful *and* witty *and* smart *and* tall as everyone had described. Bummer. Once I realized I had zero chance with her boyfriend, she
and I gradually became friends, just as everyone predicted. We
even started hanging out together way more than I ever did with
SG. I would always wonder if he had ever told her what a desperate idiot I had been when we first met. I would neurotically wonder if they would lie in bed at night, postcoital, laughing about
the little troll who thought she could come between them.

Sadly, as most trajectories go for relationships in your twenties, SG and his beautiful girlfriend eventually split. It was mutual and nothing too dramatic, but at this point I was way closer to her than him, and I had also since found myself some other loser actor to date. (This one did sort of resemble Shrek and was a total asshole. But I'm a lady so I won't discuss his wiener.)

Over the years, I remained close with the girlfriend, and she went on to find another great guy, because she's hot and that's how life works. I would still occasionally bump into SG at birthday parties or random bars. We would still flirt, and I swore he still had a little twinkle in his eye when he talked to me . . . or he was just stoned, which was also a strong possibility.

Years later, one Cinco de Mayo, I was at a friend's house party. I was very single and feeling extra confident from the combo of having broken up with my Shrek and taken up running. I had overly highlighted hair, newly toned arms, and a halter-neck dress that looked like I was competing for Miss Hawaiian Tropic. It was a perfect storm, and in walked my unicorn/SG. We locked eyes. It was one of those amazing moments where no words were spoken but, in one look, we both just knew: It. Was. On. It had been more than four years since we met, which was the longest foreplay either of us has ever or will ever experience, and there was tequila coursing through our veins. Yes, there was a moment where I thought about my girlfriend and how furious with me she would be, but I justified it with how happy she was in her new relationship. Hindsight, however, is twenty-twenty, and if the tables were turned, I definitely would have murdered young-me! I mean, how much attention and validation does a twenty-four-year-old woman need?! Welp, it turns out, a lot.

It was getting late, so I decided to say my goodbyes and make my move out of the party to see if he would follow suit. When I went to him to hug him goodbye—OMG, I will never forget this—he leaned in close and tauntingly whispered in my ear, "You're trouble." HAHAHAHAHA! I know, I know. What a line, right?? Well, it made my nether-regions tingle, so I guess it did the trick. I giggled and walked out of the party showing off the way-too-low back of my hideous halter dress.

I arrived home and no more than three minutes later, he knocked on my door. DUM DUM DUM! We proceeded to have very mediocre sex (as is most sex in your twenties), but I was grateful to finally let the air out of those tires. And, while I knew I'd never want to have sex with him again, the *guilt* of having broken girl-code like that was brutal. To this day, I have never told anyone this story . . . but I'm sure any parties involved (who read this book) will figure it out through context clues. I'm just hoping the statute of limitations has passed.

KELTIE: THE REAL WALKING DEAD

Early in my TV hosting career, I was given a very fun assignment covering the Guys Choice awards red carpet. This was an award show produced by the old cable channel SpikeTV, and based on what I saw on the red carpet, I can safely say it was all about dudes, what dudes like, and really hot chicks. The men wore T-shirts and the ladies brought out their boobs. I mean, the trophy is a golden pair of antlers . . . what more do you need to know?

This red carpet happened in 2014, when I was at the height of what I would call my biggest Keltdown ever. (Note: If you read our first book, this is around the time that I tried to crash my car into a wall.) In short, I had a health issue that was causing me to lose my hair, be depressed, and be super fuzzy and foggy. I was working crazy long hours, without many days off, and was basically a zombie shell of a human.

Normally, when I would get an assignment for a red carpet, my job was to look over the list of expected attendees and learn everything I possibly could about them. On the list of attendees there are a few categories of stars. First, there's "The Nominee." I'm talking top tier, last to arrive, biggest star, often wearing the best outfit. Next, is "The Presenter," who is lower on the chain but still important. They might be last year's winner, next year's winner, or have a super popular project in the works; their star in Hollywood is pretty shiny. Then come the stars that are on a current hit show but have no reason to be at the event. This level star is either trying to extend their fifteen minutes of fame or their kid wants to be there. They also might be trying to meet another celebrity that is supposed to be in attendance. This happens a lot at music events where TV actors will bring their kids just to meet a popstar ('cause the kids don't think Dad being on TV is cool, but they really like Justin Bieber and want to meet him). Finally, low, low, low on the list are the hanger-on Hollywood types who are just coming to be "seen" on the red carpet. They are either brand new to the scene and have a great publicist who wants them to be photographed in nice outfits at events. Or, they can't get a job and are trying to make the rounds at cool events to drum up some thirst. FYI: Hollywood is awful. I also want to mention that at the very bottom of this pecking order is *me*. I walk the red carpet before anyone actually gets there so it looks like I went to the event, but I only stood outside interviewing people. FYI: I've "been" to the Met Gala six times, but I've never actually been inside.

When you watch an entertainment news show or see an article online, it usually features two or three of the top celebrity stories from that event. However, the guest list can go anywhere from 25 stars at a small event to 250 stars during the six-hour Grammy red carpet! To snag the standout interviews on the carpet, my job as a reporter was to get that list of possible carpet walkers, research their current and previous projects, and think of distinctive questions for each of them. The Spike TV Guys Choice red carpet happened to fall on a Saturday, when I had already worked the entire week and was definitely taking a ride on the struggle bus as far as life goes. I was feeling so low and so stressed and so tired that I did something that I never did before (or again) in my decade-long reporting career: I decided I could just "wing it." I didn't have the time to do my normal deep dive into each star, and since it was sort of a fun and lighthearted event (Guys! Hot girls! Chicken wings! Boobs!), I figured that I knew enough about the vibe to do the interviews cold. Bad idea.

The red carpet began, and I was excited to start my night with Chrissy Teigen, who was just beginning her meteoric rise at the time. She was quite literally the most exciting thing in Hollywood and was doing tons of interviews. She wore this little yellow mini dress and was all big hair and personality, fresh, outspoken, and so nice! We chatted for a good ten minutes, and when she walked away from my interview I thought, *Well, there's our story*, and patted myself on the back.

Next on the list was Jessica Alba, which was a big deal because she rarely does interviews. I was apparently blinded by my excitement to snag this rare interview because what happened next was the biggest career fail of my life. In line, in front of Jessica on the red carpet, was a man with shaggy, emo-like hair, dressed in a nondescript black blazer. When his publicist approached me and asked if I'd like to do an interview I quipped, "I'm sorry, we are staying open for Jessica," who was next in line to walk the carpet. The publicist looked shocked, mentioned their guy was winning the top award, and asked me again. I said no, again. The publicist was upset, but any publicity team is going to be salty when you turn down their client, so I didn't think much of this moment. Remember, I was in the middle of a health crisis, four follicles away from being bald, with such bad inflammation that the sight in my left eye was gone . . . I was basically "walking dead" at this point in my week. So I moved on, got my interview with the gorgeous Jessica, and that was a wrap. I changed out of my heels and into my flip-flops and walked back to my car. I was driving home, exhausted, not thinking much about my work that day when I got a phone call from a high-up producer at my show demanding to know: "Why did you pass on Norman Reedus?"

In the iconic words of Keke Palmer, "I hate to say it . . . I don't know who this man is . . . he could be walking down the street, I wouldn't know a thing. . . . Sorry to this man."

I did not know who this Norman man was. Allegedly *The Walking Dead* was the biggest show on television at the time, and Norman Reedus was its biggest male star, garnering the main award of the whole night. And I had no idea who he was because I was the idiot who had barely scanned my paperwork, not done my research, and passed on interviewing him.

Something you need to know about me. I stick to a strict "brain diet." I don't consume things that upset me or are violent at all. The scariest movie I've ever seen in my life is *Avengers*. I kid you not, that is the level of fighting and things being blown up that I can take before I melt down and have nightmares so awful you'd never want to go to sleep again in your life. I've never seen a scary movie, and I refuse to watch anything with guns, guts, or gore. So, obviously, I have never seen a single episode of *The Walking Dead*. If I someday make it to the pearly gates of Heaven and God turns to me and says, "Tell me one thing about *The Walking Dead*," I will have to turn around and head to Hell. *That* is my level of familiarity with the show.

So, what does an eager, young, perfectionist reporter (who has messed up majorly but doesn't want her bosses to know she's a straight-up idiot) do? I did what any overworked, over-glammed, over-her-head woman does when there is truly *no other option.*

I blamed it on my period.

I told the producers that, in that moment, I had just realized my period was leaking down my bare leg and was dealing with that, which was why I was flustered and passed on *obviously* Norman Reedus. Yes, I did. Furthermore, in the process of fixing the relationship with Norman's team after my fuckup, I had to repeat this lie multiple times to multiple people that I respect and would never normally lie to. I'm also a horrible liar, so now that the truth is out, I am expecting many "we knew you were lying" texts from those people. This is a secret I have thought about every single time I do the weekly dusting of my three Entertainment News Emmy Awards. I have been burdened by my fake period for years! I feel so free now that the world knows!

I also want to personally apologize to Norman. Many people enjoy you, sir, and you seem like a nice person from what I've googled. Let me add that I've always enjoyed razor haircuts on men, so kudos to you on your style. I heard you were excellent in your show that featured blood baths, and I am truly sorry that I lied about mine.

Also, please google Keltie Knight 2014 Spike Guys Choice awards for a visual. Sorry, Normie!

LADYGANG CONFESSIONS

SOCK IT POO YA!

I went to dinner in Marina del Rey with a guy whom I'd been seeing. I had just lost a little bit of weight, and I was feeling myself, but my belly had been doing some really funky things to my intestines for days. After dinner my date was like, "Oh God, you look so great, blah blah blah." We went back to his boat, this gorgeous forty-footer, that he kept in the marina. Upon arrival, I took a minute in the bathroom to freshen up, and when I peed, I noticed the toilet didn't flush. Having worked on a few boats myself, I knew they sometimes flushed differently at sea than on land, but nothing I tried seemed to work, so the thing must have been broken. We had sex and fell asleep. I woke up bright and early at 6:00 a.m., like I always do, to the beautiful sight of the UCLA crew team. Standing there on the boat watching them, I was butt naked, enjoying the view when I felt a gurgling wave in my stomach. A wave like I was going to *die*.

Sidenote: I used to crash the pool at the Marina del Rey Hotel all the time, so thankfully I knew the area. Because when this wave hit, I had about ten seconds to throw my clothes on and find a way to deal with the impending "shit-uation" without using the broken toilet. I threw on my short black tank dress, grabbed my motorcycle boots, and these fuzzy socks I'd been wearing the night before because the boots were a little big. It was absolute go time. I told him I'll be right back and took off down the dock toward the pool so I could hop the fence and use their bathroom. As I was running down the dock, there was diarrhea coming out of my butt so I did what any sane person would do and, holding my boots in one hand, I used a fuzzy sock to catch my poop as best I could.

I finally got to that bathroom, peeled off my dress, and there was shit up my back. It was just a next-level horror show. At the time, I smoked, so I lit up a cigarette and just stood in the stall, chain-smoking naked, trying to figure out how I was going to get the shit smell off me. I had 3% battery on my phone, I couldn't call an Uber, and I needed to grab my purse back on the boat. It was one of those worst-case scenarios. Thankfully, the bathroom was empty so I washed my dress in the sink and tried to dry it under the hand dryer. My socks went straight into the trash. I left the bathroom, got back to the boat, and couldn't find the guy. For like an hour, I searched the marina, and he finally reappeared. My dress was still damp, but all he could do was tell me how great I looked. He wanted to grab a coffee, but I just wanted to get out of there before the next wave hit me. I didn't want to sit down either, because my dress might make a huge wet spot on the cushions. I was just praying for it to be over. I managed to get out of there, terrified that he noticed that I smelled like actual shit. He called later, and I didn't want to pick up, convinced he was calling to tell me he'd realized what had happened. Somehow, it was never revealed that I'd nearly had a blowout on his boat, but lesson learned. Always carry baby wipes and extra perfume in your bag because you never know when you might get hit with a wave and must shit in a fuzzy sock.

RIP TURBO

I met this really cute guy out at a bar one night. We got to talking and realized we actually had some friends in common, and, after a few drinks, I decided he was prime one-night-stand material. After a while, we decided to head back to his place. It's your standard single-guy apartment, nothing too fancy, but the first thing I noticed was his super cute dog. We were making out a bit in his living room, and it was fine, but I kind of just wanted to play with that dog! Things started to get hot and heavy, and we moved into his bedroom. The dog followed us, and sort of stood at the foot of the bed and watched as we took our clothes off. It was actually pretty funny. Apparently, the pup was just super loyal and had some separation anxiety. We went at it, and I pretended the pup wasn't there. We fell asleep, the pup in between us (the little guy snored! It was charming), and the next morning, I woke up before anyone did to make a quick exit.

Except, when I went rooting around on the floor for all my clothes, I couldn't, for the life of me, find my underwear. It was so bizarre. I didn't really want to extend things though, so after a few minutes of slightly frantic searching, I kind of figured it was only a pair of panties, and I might as well just leave without them. I grabbed the rest of my stuff, gave the pup a scratch under the chin, and went on with my life. I never heard from the guy and I never texted him, but a few weeks later, I found out from a mutual friend that he had a girlfriend, so that made me feel a little sketchy. I also found out that his dog had passed away. I actually felt bad about that one. When I asked what happened, I wished I hadn't. Apparently, the dog had died from an obstruction in his intestines. The obstruction? *My underwear*. Rest in peace, Turbo.

> I went through my boyfriend's phone when we were fighting, thinking I would find something terrible. Instead, I found texts to a jeweler about an engagement ring. My boyfriend had even sent pictures from my Pinterest of the ring he knew I was obsessed with. I'm an ass.

YOU CAN'T CATCH A NEW DOG WITH OLD TRICKS

I had this ex. I broke up with him. Actually, it was mutual. Okay, let's be real, he broke up with me and I was really not prepared. Kind of an out-of-left-field, out-of-the-blue situation. Needless to say, it really tore me up, and I was definitely *not* over him. After wallowing for a few days, crying into some ice cream, re-watching all our favorite movies, crying into some more ice cream, and generally feeling miserable, I started to plot different ways to see him. Of course, immediately post breakup, the scenarios I started to cook up in my head went from probable to plausible to downright insane pretty quickly. Forget the numerous ways we could casually "run into each other" in the market we used to frequent outside our favorite coffee shop, or at a bar with friends, or have any other sort of normal encounter. In my infinite post-breakup sadness, my imagination spun out all kinds of ways to get him to call me, all sorts of emergency situations that would require his help, and even crafted some Oscar-worthy *Notebook*-style reconciliations.

Of course, none of those came to fruition, and as my dream of a rain-soaked reunion seemed ever more unlikely, I did the most sane thing I could think of—I kidnapped his dog. Yep, you read that correctly. When all other plots failed, I took matters into my own hands and snuck over to his house when I knew he'd be out. I'd always loved his dog (yet another reason the breakup really hurt), and the little guy was happy to see me. I kept an eye out for any nosy neighbors and squirreled him to my car. I thought about staging a sighting and texting my ex a photo (carefully posed, of course, so I looked particularly good in my hiking shorts) from an imaginary trek to show him it was, in fact, his dog. I thought about letting him freak out for a few days and then showing up at his door in a similarly well-planned outfit, dog in hand, as if I'd just happened upon him. Instead, I left him a voicemail explaining that I'd found his dog wandering in the hills, which I figured wouldn't be too much of a stretch since we'd gone hiking there quite a few times with the dog when we were together. I'm not going to lie, I was unhinged. After all, I'd dognapped the poor creature, and it wasn't like he had the habit of escaping. I worried that my ex would see straight through it and send me away for good. Of course, he called back (man's best friend and all) and thanked me profusely for finding him. I arranged to come over to his place to drop the pup back to him, and he invited me to stay for dinner. We laughed and talked well into the night, just as I'd hoped, but said our eventual, final goodbyes in the end. While we didn't last, I still think about that dog a lot. Poor thing—why on earth did I involve him?

WHAT HAPPENS IN VEGAS GETS STASHED IN THE SAND

Over a decade ago I was at the Hard Rock Hotel pool party, Rehab, in Las Vegas. If you have never seen the reality TV show about these parties, let me enlighten you. The hotel used to throw these ragers every Sunday, and the vibe at the pool, which looked like a beach, was like a big spring break event. There were DJs, minor celebrities, cabanas you could rent, potential undercover sting operations. It was peak 2000s. There I was, looking fine as hell, getting drunk with my girls, music blasting. These parties were seriously fun, full of hot people, and definitely not the classiest, but we were young, in Vegas, and looking for an epic time. That's when I met a guy I wanted to bang. I also happened to be on my period, so I did what any drunk girl would do! I took out my tampon in the water and buried it in the sand in the beach area that covered the pool deck. Not deterred by the fact the party was packed, or the fact there were tons of strangers around us and my friends were only about ten feet away, I attempted pool sex in the middle of the chaos. It still haunts me that someone probably stepped on my used tampon and unearthed it, causing it to float on the surface of that crowded pool.

I'VE BEEN WITH MY BF FOR FOUR YEARS. FAKED EVERY. SINGLE. TIME.

THE THERA-*PISSED*

I had been seeing a therapist for intimacy issues for about two years. Fear of attachment, anxiety, avoidance, self-loathing, the whole nine yards. I was finally at a point where I was addressing all that super fun stuff that clogs up your emotional ability to just be a "normal" person, go out on a date, and not totally freak out. It was great. I'd found a therapist I really liked, and for a commitment-phobe like me, finding (and committing to!) any kind of relationship was hard. After months of hard self-work, I was really digging into the root of some of my problems. My therapist was fantastic, and I was starting to feel like maybe, just maybe, I'd found the woman who might be able to help me in the long term. So, of course, I decided to put all that time and hard work to the test. I went out and met a guy.

First date, good. Didn't bring him home. It seemed like we had a good rapport, and I was nervous, but excited, to see him again. Second date, even better. Still didn't bring him home. I was starting to hope, just a bit, that I'd finally turned a page. I'd used the tools my therapist had given me and managed to make it all the way to date three. I'm not one of those women that has "rules" about how many dates I wait, but I'd followed her advice and taken it one step at a time. Of course, partway through date three, all those healthy boundaries went right out the window. The vibe was just different. We both drank *a lot*, and I ended up taking him home. Things got hot and heavy and, well, intimate. However, afterward, he left in a rush with barely a glance or a goodbye. Surprise, surprise, that was the last I saw or heard from him. Back to the couch I went.

A few months later, when COVID hit, my therapist chose to work out of her home for the foreseeable future. One day, I was on camera and she placed the computer in the hallway, which she was using as a waiting room outside her home office. While waiting, I caught the sight of a man making food in the adjacent kitchen. Guess who? The same man—my Mr. Disappear-Without-a-Trace-and-Couldn't-Even-Text-Back date. What in the world was he doing there, you ask? Oh, he lived there. Why? *He was her husband.*

NATIONAL FUCKIN' (AROUND) LEAGUE

I had a three-year affair with an NFL player, starting during his engagement and lasting two years into his marriage. I didn't know he was engaged when we met, and we dated six months before his wedding aired on ESPN, which totally gave away his secret. I could've walked away then but I didn't . . . our relationship ended a few months ago, amicably.

THE SCHOLAR-*SHIT*

One day in junior year of high school, I was having horrible stomach pains every hour or so. During the last half hour of the school day, I was sitting in English class and very suddenly had to use the bathroom. I wasn't going to make it though, and before I could do anything about it, I sharted my pants right then and there while sitting at my desk. Luckily the shart didn't make any noise, but after a couple minutes the stench filled the entire room, and the air was rancid. The rest of the class kept looking around trying to figure out where the smell was coming from so I joined in and did the same. I was a straight A student and fairly soft-spoken, so no one really suspected me of committing such a foul crime in the middle of a discussion on *The Great Gatsby*. As soon as the bell rang, I jog-walked to the restroom and had to throw out my undies (thankfully my jeans were unharmed). To this day, no one in that English class knows the perpetrator of the shart. It was me . . . the eventual valedictorian of my class.

I'm twenty-nine years old
and I still suck my thumb
to fall asleep.

SEVEN-YEAR SITCH

My husband and I started dating when we were in high school. During my senior year of college, we broke up temporarily for about a year. During that time, I drunkenly had sex with his now best friend. After we stopped, my now-hubby and I got back together. That's when he and that friend became attached at the hip. Absolute besties. This man was the best man in our wedding, and I became really good friends with his wife. The four of us go on vacation together all the time, and it's just a big dark secret the two of us have. Neither of our spouses has ever found out. Sometimes, my husband will randomly ask me, "Did you hook up with anyone that I wouldn't want to know about when we were not together?" Every time he asks, I cringe. We've been married for seven years, back together for nine. I will take it to my grave, and I just pray to God that the friend can keep his trap shut as well!

HAMSLAUGHTER

I used to have a job working in the homes of adults with acquired brain injuries. One of my clients had a hamster as a family pet. This client loved that hamster *so much*, which makes this that much worse. The hamster had sort of morphed into this tiny emotional support animal, in addition to helping its owner regain the fine motor skills needed to hold small things. I am not a huge fan of rodents, so often when the client encouraged me to hold the hamster, I would politely decline.

One day, the client was particularly insistent, so I felt obligated and held the hamster in my hands. The client left the room for a few minutes, and everything seemed fine. The hamster and I sort of stared at each other. Then, the unthinkable happened. After looking me dead in the face, this tiny ball of fur leapt out of my hands and dropped to the floor. It vaulted itself off my palm and into the great pet cemetery in the sky. It was like it happened in slow motion. The hamster fell, and my eyes bugged out of my head as I watched it go down. Rest in peace, little ball of fur. I panicked. I was horrified and didn't know what to do. I quickly picked it up, dropped it back in the cage, and was literally sweating as I tried to figure out what to say.

The client walked back into the room, saw the hamster in its cage, not moving, and I just prayed he wouldn't freak out. Luckily, nothing dramatic happened. The client just said the hamster was super old and probably died of natural causes, but I knew the truth. I've never told anyone, and, to this day, I just wait for that lightning bolt to strike me down every time I think about it. I am a monster.

I OFTEN THINK ABOUT MY LIFE AFTER MY HUSBAND PASSES AWAY AND HOW IT WOULD BE A GREAT BACKSTORY AS A CONTESTANT ON *THE BACHELOR*.

THE CLIMB-AX

When I was in elementary school, I would climb the rope in gym class or at recess, and I would get tingly feelings "down there." Obviously at that age I had no idea what was happening. As I got older (still in elementary school), it started to feel even better, and I would climb the rope every chance I got. Sometimes it would even end *really well*, and I'd have to play it cool in front of everyone when I was done. I did this often, even throughout junior high. It wasn't until my first orgasm by a guy in high school that I realized what was happening to me every time I climbed the rope. Pretty sure I've had more orgasms as a child climbing that rope than I've had with men as an adult.

SNAPPED CHAT

My husband and I decided to refinish the side tables in our bedroom. We were out in the garage, sanding down the tables, blasting music, and having some cocktails. Genuinely having a good time. Halfway through sanding my table, I decided it was time for another drink and some new music. So, I picked up my husband's phone and changed the song. As I changed the song, I realized there was a Snapchat notification from a woman whose name I didn't recognize. I paused for a minute and thought about what I should do. Should I ignore it and think about it all day every day for the next several weeks or open it and feel guilty about snooping even though my gut said I just might have a good reason to? I chose the latter.

As I opened the notification, the first thing I saw was a kissy emoji, which was enough to validate my feelings about going through his phone. Let me just say now, I am not one to snoop. I never have been and I'm not pleased that I did. *But,* in hindsight, it was the best decision I've ever made. As I scrolled up through their chat conversation, I saw saved photos that were sexual in nature and coming from both parties. Her boobs out in a tanning bed, him pulling his pants down past his hip to show his "abs" or whatever . . . and so on. You get the picture.

At this point, I was *fuming.* A thousand thoughts went through my mind. Do I lose my shit? Do I punch him in the throat? Or . . . do I act like I didn't see anything and be a total psycho? Bingo. Option number three. So, I calmly changed the song and went on with my night. The next thing I know, I'm suggesting tequila shots. But, of course, the shots were for him. Little did he know, I didn't drink anything but water. This was fairly easy to pull off, as I love tequila, and I have a much higher tolerance for alcohol than he does. I didn't even have to put on much of a show.

Sure enough, after a couple of hours, he's face deep in the toilet, puking. Perfect. Now I could get down to business. I pulled out his phone to see what was really going on. I went through the rest of the Snapchat conversation, only to find more photos over the years. I was devastated. So, I decided to do what I thought was the most impactful, satisfying, and bitchy thing I could think of. I printed every single photo that I found from the Snapchat conversation, compiled my evidence, and placed it on my pillow in the bedroom.

I went to sleep in the bed in the spare room but didn't manage to sleep for even two seconds. He came into the room early the next morning, hungover as hell, confused as to why I wasn't sleeping with him. Clearly, he didn't roll over to see the stack of K-type documents I'd left for him on my pillow. I told him to go back to the bedroom and try again. The rest is history. I've never told anyone that I got him blackout drunk so that I could strip-search his phone for evidence. It feels pretty damn good to get off my chest.

I SNOOZE, YOU LOSE

You know how sometimes, no matter how much you love your spouse, you find yourself doing bizarre things because his family, your in-laws, have the potential to drive you up a wall? Well, when I am with my husband's family for an extended time, and I just need a break so as not to lose my mind, I pretend to sleep. I pretend to sleep anywhere. I have "fallen asleep" at the dinner table in a restaurant. I've slept at college football games, concerts, family reunions, wakes, Thanksgivings, you name it. My mother-in-law always tells people, "This girl can sleep anywhere!" She'll then proceed to name all the aforementioned places, and more, that I have done so, shaking her head in disbelief. I've been doing this for over twelve years now to get a quiet minute to myself, and they all remain in absolute awe of my great sleeping abilities.

"
I think my
husband has
a small penis,
but I love
him anyway.
"

THE SISTER SHOCKER

Ah, the beautiful miracle of life. Well, here's what no one really prepares you for—giving birth can have some decidedly, shall we say, less than beautiful results. Case in point: I was super constipated after having my son and also had some small hemorrhoids. About two weeks postpartum, I was so backed up and uncomfortable, I was willing to do anything to get relief. I tried eating fiber supplements, took laxatives, inserted a suppository, nothing was working. Every time I tried to poop, I was just pushing and pushing and nothing would come out. I was pushing so hard I almost made myself pass out. I thought I was going to burst the stitches down there. It was bad. It legit felt like I was walking around with a *giant* hard dick in my butt. My twin sister, who is a nurse, happened to be staying with me while this was all going down. She kept telling me to put gloves on, lube them up, and stick my fingers up there. Well, I couldn't quite grasp what she was trying to explain to me, so she took matters into her own hands (quite literally) and did it for me. Yep—my twin sister stuck her fingers up my ass for me. Once she did, I felt *immediate* relief. Absolutely life changing. It honestly almost felt better than giving birth. And it just goes to show that sisters will do anything for each other.

NOT SO OVER EASY

As a seven-year-old, I found a robin's nest with five tiny turquoise eggs. I thought I could raise one of the eggs, so I took one inside. I made it a comfortable home in a shoebox with some tissues. I remembered learning that mama birds sat on the eggs to keep them warm. My logical conclusion was that more heat = faster growth. I placed this tiny turquoise egg in my microwave and cooked it for a few minutes. I don't recall how long before the loud explosion inside of the microwave. It was a murder scene inside . . . exploded blood and bits all over my grandmother's microwave. I was devastated by what I did. I cleaned it up to hide the evidence. I've never told this to any human. I have told my fiancé *every* dirty, dark secret I have. He'll never know that I'm a bird killer.

I HAD SEX WITH THE LEAD SINGER OF THIRD EYE BLIND.

SNITCH SITCH

I used to log in to my boyfriend's Instagram daily and read all of his DMs. Not necessarily the healthiest way to go about a relationship, but most of the time, they were pretty harmless. While I wouldn't recommend snooping on someone else's social media, we'd always trusted each other to the point of knowing things like passcodes and certain account login information. Unfortunately, I was definitely the only one taking advantage. He wasn't really big into social media at all, but he did have this one group chat with his close guy friends. Usually, it was your standard locker room talk fare of male bravado and inside jokes that could semi-border on nonsensical. Mostly just ribbing on one another, reminding someone to pick up beers, rehashing something that happened during college, or making fun of one of the single guys for his escapades. Of course, snoop long enough, and you'll find something, right? One time, I logged in, and there in the group chat was this message from one of his oldest and closest friends. Let's call him Tom. Tom happened to be in a long-term relationship with a really great girl (let's call her Kate). Kate was one of my best friends. The four of us did fun couple things, and Kate and I hung out a lot, bonded by our mutual love of this goofy group of guys. Plenty of wine nights, even a few of our own inside jokes. Us girls had to stick together, and I think that's why this was so awful. Tom had sent a message to the guys saying he'd "fucked the girl with the huge tits" the night before. What's worse, none of the guys called him out on it. They just sort of laughed it off, congratulated him, and moved on. Tom told them not to tell anyone and asked them to delete the message after they read it. I don't know if my boyfriend deleted it or not, but he definitely saw it, because the message had been read by the time I was creeping around in his inbox. I've known this secret for almost two years, and I can't tell my boyfriend, because I was lurking on his social media like a *psycho*, and he'd definitely be horrified at the prospect of me digging through his DMs. Because of the deceptive way I found out, I can't tell Kate either, even though I think she deserves to know. Basically, I'm sitting on the ticking bomb that would ruin my relationship and probably ruin all our friendships. I feel so shitty every time I think about it.

'CUZ I LOVE HIM

I'm twenty-two and my cousin is twenty-four. My entire life I have thought he was the hottest thing since sliced bread. It was a joke when I was little and now it's weird, but I don't care. He has beautiful brown curly hair, runs marathons, and rides motorcycles. Whenever I see him post on Instagram I get excited like I'm seeing my crush post. I know it's awful, but I can't help it.

THE BATTERIES ARE DEAD

My boyfriend's dad passed away, and right after the funeral, my boyfriend (who is now my ex, by the way) and his mom had to go out of town for a while so he asked me to house-sit. I was happy to help in any way I could. He mentioned that it would be fine to have people over as long as we didn't leave anything behind that his mom would notice. A few days into my stay, I was bored, so I invited a few guy friends over, and we ended up snooping around. It's kind of fun to snoop around someone's house when they aren't there (you know you've done it, too!). While in his mom's bedroom, we opened up a few drawers and found a vibrator. Long story short, I ended up letting both of them use it on me. On my boyfriend's mom's bed. It was hot, but when they left, I had to wash that vibrator and put it back in her dead husband's sock drawer. I cringe, even today, thinking about it.

I slept with BFF's BF.
The dick was trash.

LIAR'S LICENSE

A few years ago, I accompanied my boyfriend on a work trip. On the last evening, we attended a formal company event. We got all dressed up (and looked pretty great, I must admit), and I gave my boyfriend my ID to hold during dinner. Why, oh why, don't all formal dresses have pockets? As the night progressed, we were having a great time and proceeded to get pretty hammered. Open bar, hilarious coworkers, feeling like we're on vacation, the whole nine yards. We had to fly out early the next morning, so, hungover and stressed, we woke up only to realize my ID was missing. I swore he had put it in his suit coat pocket; he swore he gave it back to me. We went back and forth on it for hours. It morphed into this giant blow-up fight and remains by far the worst argument I've ever had with a man. I was convinced he'd lost it sometime in the evening; he was convinced he'd handed it back before we left the event. Then it wasn't just about the ID anymore, but about being aware, taking responsibility, being mature. Basically, an airing of all sorts of grievances.

Eventually, we headed to the airport without it. I don't know what it is about airports but they initiate this bizarre, almost Pavlovian response where, as soon as people walk in, they become the worst versions of themselves. Or lose all reason. Or both. We had to jump through a million hoops to get me on a plane with no valid photo ID. I had to go into a separate room, prove who I was by giving them a full autobiography and the promise of my first-born child. Then there was the pat down, and my bag was taken apart piece by piece and searched. As in, each individual tampon in my makeup bag was picked up and inspected. Keep in mind, we were still extremely hungover, and the whole time I was bitching at him for losing my ID. I truly don't know how we made it on and off that flight without breaking up. Well, two weeks later I found the ID in a small pocket in my suitcase. Turns out he'd been right all along. He'd given it back to me at some point in the evening, and I had, in my alcohol-induced state, stashed it in my own bag. Talk about taking responsibility. We were living together, so I did the supremely mature thing—I cut the ID into tiny pieces and threw it into a dumpster about five miles from our apartment so he would never find it. It's been four years and we're married now . . . he will never know the truth.

BROTHER FUCKER

In 2014 my best friend and I were both fresh out of a pair of nasty breakups with the most dreadful men on the planet. We decided to make ourselves feel better and booked an all-inclusive trip to Cuba. At the airport, we met a bachelor party waiting for the same flight that we were boarding. They asked us to take a few photos of the group, so we started to chat with them and found out they were staying at the same resort as us. My bestie and I gave each other the eyes . . . we were stoked. We'd met a nice group of slightly douchey, super hot men. They were absolutely the perfect candidates for some fun rebound vacation sex. Excellent for getting over our exes. Something that would ultimately go nowhere but could contribute to great memories in our twenties that we could look back on and laugh about in our eighties.

Now, there was a pair of brothers in the group. I got the older one and my friend got the younger one. We'd all hit it off at the hotel bar, and the two of us both did the dirty on night one (and on nights two through seven). As the week went on, we got to know them both a little bit better. The younger one, who my friend was cuffing, was our age and a total sweetheart. He was so funny and fun to hang with. I immediately felt like I had known him for years. His brother, on the other hand, was the exact opposite. He was a total douche, didn't give a shit about getting to know us, and just wanted to bang and send me on my way. As in "wham, bam, thank you ma'am!" He would literally kick me out of the room every night as soon as we were done. At the time I was fine with that because I wasn't looking for my soulmate, but, nonetheless, he sucked.

We never thought we would see these guys again, so we made up fake stories about our lives and had a good time with it. We had an awesome week, and when it was time to say goodbye, we played it cool and took off without any of their personal info.

Fast-forward to about three months later, when I opened my Facebook account to a message from the younger brother. He had just moved to a neighboring town and decided to look me up. At first, I thought he was getting me and my bestie confused because he didn't add or message her. After chatting for a little, he explained that he had actually been interested in me all along, but his brother had gotten in the way. He went on to say that he had been thinking of me ever since the trip and figured he might as well shoot his shot.

My best friend swore she wasn't interested in him and ended up back with her toxic ex anyway. Still, girl code and all, I was pretty apprehensive about it for months, but the conversations we were having were like nothing I had ever had with anyone. We clicked instantly. My best friend encouraged me to go for it, and after months of him asking me out, I finally accepted. Seven years later, and we are married and expecting our first child together. We are still so in love and he really is my soulmate. It took me a solid year to face his douchey brother, and it was extremely awkward for quite a long time. Strangely, it wasn't ever awkward at all between my best friend and my husband. Everyone thinks that we met in Cuba and fell in love instantly . . . little do they know I've banged my brother-in-law and my husband banged my best friend. There were multiple mentions during our wedding speeches about falling in love in Cuba, and to this day only the four of us know the truth.

CELWYDDOG, CELWYDDOG!

I went to an elite university in western Europe. It was truly like something out of a movie. Gorgeous medieval buildings, amazing nightlife, a drinking age of eighteen, and the most beautiful people. While everything was nearly perfect, there was one thing that drove me to do something a little insane. Immediately upon arriving there, I became incredibly insecure about my language abilities. Or rather, lack thereof. Everyone around me could speak multiple languages, and here I was, able to speak only English. I'm not talking the casual, conversational, "I did three years of French in high school" or "I spent a summer in Barcelona" type of language speaking either. They were fully fluent. We're talking four, five, six languages, sometimes even more. I spent an inordinate amount of time being really worried about it. Not wanting to seem uncultured and uncool, what did I do? I pretended I could speak Welsh. Yes, that's right. Welsh. With so few fluent speakers outside, well, Wales (I think there's about a million people who actually speak it), I sort of figured I would never be tested on it. It also contains words like "cwdyn" and "spigoglys," and also has the longest town name, *Llanfairpwllgwyngyllgogerychwyrndrobwllllantysiliogogogoch*, so you see how, in the land of fairly snotty polyglots, it was easy to fudge it, just a bit. At first, I didn't think it was really a big thing, but I was surprised at how well it worked. It also gave me this weird sort of credibility. Instead of stressing over pretending to speak another language, I should have been actually *learning* another language rather than just making one up. The problem is, recently, I've sort of had to back it up more and more. When I talk to my parents, I pretend to speak Welsh so my friends don't think I am lying. Obviously, they haven't picked up on the fact that I'm honestly bullshitting every single word. Literally just making sounds up. The lie has gone so far now that I live in fear of the day a native speaker will appear out of nowhere and expose me, and I'm going to be known as "that girl." It's honestly terrifying.

PETTY CASHING IN

I've worked for my company for fifteen years, and I used to be in control of the safe where we kept all the cash. My job was to count our petty cash every day, and then I would document the total count. If there was a day the amount was over what I'd have to put back, I would pocket the difference. This is something I'm 100% *not* proud of, and actually very ashamed of myself for doing. Although it's not an excuse, my reasoning for doing so was that I was in an extremely hard spot in my life. I was in a toxic, awful relationship, was constantly manipulated, and was forced to move in with my boyfriend. I had no money, could not afford my portion of rent, and was overdrawing my bank account all the time. I never let on to anyone that I was having a hard time, so I'm assuming that is why they never suspected it. As soon as I got into a better spot, I stopped. But man, that petty cash just about saved my life.

PART TWO

WELL, THIS IS AWKWARD

Cringy Confessions That Make Us Want to Disappear Forever

You know when you're lying in bed, slowly drifting off to sleep, and your brain decides it's the *perfect* time to remind you of "that one time" you got a vibrator stuck up your butt, or you tried to become besties with your boyfriend's ex (that's considered light stalking, BTW), or you got caught stealing some poker chips from an Olympic hero? A memory of something so cringe and humiliating that your stomach drops, your adrenaline spikes, your eyes fly open, and you start wishing your mattress would just swallow you whole? Of course you do, you're one of us!

At the end of the day, these kinds of secrets all boil down to shame, don't they? As our emotional guru Brené Brown brilliantly said, "Shame is the intensely painful feeling or experience of believing that we are flawed and therefore unworthy of love and belonging." Every single one of us has said or done something we regret, only to be haunted by the embarrassment of our actions for years and years after everyone else involved has forgotten. The more we beat ourselves up about our flaws, the tighter we hold on to that guilt. The tighter we hold on to our guilt, the worse we feel as a person. And the worse we feel as a person, the more we beat ourselves up. It's a super fun self-loathing hamster wheel of shame!

Keeping secrets, no matter how small or stupid, makes us feel isolated. So allow us to help you feel less alone. After reading through thousands of mortifying submissions, we started to see some patterns emerge. Turns out, we are *all* having problems with our vaginas. A bunch of vageniuses we are not. We are constantly getting random objects stuck up there, forgetting things we *purposely* put in, and in at least one case you're about to read about, finding a living creature hanging out in there. We are constantly caring for UTIs and yeast infections and ingrown hairs and HPV and a million other things that throw off our very delicate pH balance. It's ironic, because our vaginas are the *literal* source of life, but goddamn they are fragile little bitches.

Secondly, sex is messy, and mixing body fluids with another person, whether it's the first time or you've been riding their pony for a decade, comes with risks. The noises, the accidents, and the "ouch that's my butthole" are all part of making whoopee. We love that our ladies are willing to take risks and experiment on their way to Pleasure Town (and we hear it's across the street from Flavor Town). And we hope when you get there, you are greeted with the Big O.

And lastly, surprisingly, not everything cringy has to do with our lady parts. The collective message of "oh my god I cannot believe I did that" is universal. When we say "disappear forever," we really mean collectively screaming "NOOOOOOO!" with a dropped jaw at our next brunch over mimosas. (Pls don't disappear, we love you!) Secrets so humiliating, so stomach-dropping, so unbelievable that we stop scrolling on our Instagram to give you our uninterrupted focus. These are the ones that made us shudder with secondhand embarrassment as we were reading them.

Whatever your unspeakable secret is, chances are one of these stories is worse. And you can rest easy knowing you're not alone in these life-ruining, slowly-back-into-a-bush-like-Homer-Simpson moments.

So, here we say *own your shit* (literally and figuratively) and stop hiding in the awkward crawl spaces of life. The only thing that determines how much shame you feel about something (and for how long you feel it) is you. Sleep well knowing that the humiliating story from fifteen years ago that keeps you up at night is just a teeny little blip in everyone else's memory. The most valuable lesson you can learn in your short time on this planet is that everyone's head is so far up their own ass that they aren't even thinking about you. So get out there and do whatever the fuck you want (within reason!).

JAC: $4,000 LAXATIVE

I am usually a very carefree, spontaneous person, but there is one thing in my life that is extremely regimented: my morning pooping ritual. I'm not a natural pooper and I need constant assistance to feel remotely regular. Through my adult years, I have perfected my morning routine to rev up the digestive system and force my body to expel all of the French fries and chocolate chip cookies that I consume on a daily basis. There are a lot of moving pieces that have to line up perfectly for a satisfying poop, and if one thing is even a litttttttttle off center, I miss my chance and my whole day is ruined from the get-go. Y'know, I'm not a regular gal, I'm a constipated gal! So, here are a few things that *must* be in line for a poop to happen:

Sleep in my own bed

Take a magnesium citrate at bedtime

Go to bed before 11:00 p.m. and have a decent sleep

Don't be hungover

Wake up between 7:00 and 7:30 a.m.

Take a probiotic

Chug a glass of water

Drink one cup of coffee in bed uninterrupted for 45 minutes

And then if I'm lucky . . . poop

I know what you're thinking. This "ritual" is very mild and very doable, right? Well, nothing is as easy as it seems, my friends. Something as simple as having to wake up at 6:30 instead of 7:00, or having one too many glasses of wine, or running out of magnesium, or my fiancé waking up early and blabbing about his dream about being born and "wiggling through the birth canal" throws a complete wrench in the mix, and then I'm totally fucked for the day.

But the one thing that *really* screws me up is . . . traveling. And partying. And vacation. And partying *on* vacation. Basically, all my favorite things in the world! Ugh, why must you do this to me, cruel, cruel world?!

So, this story begins on a Fourth of July trip to Phoenix with a group of friends. The first morning of our vacation, I woke up with a super sour stomach, but I couldn't poop, so this rancid feeling just sat in my belly like a rotten brick. My fiancé eventually ran to the store and bought me some Pepto Bismol (like the sweetie pie he is), and I started chomping on those fuckers like they were Adderall in 2009. I probably should have googled side effects, but I was so concerned with trying not to hurl at dinner that I didn't really care. Spoiler alert: Pepto Bismol makes you constipated as shit (literally, though). I didn't poop for four days. And I raged my face off during those four days. So by the end of the trip, I was filled to the brim with chicken fingers, Bud Light, and Fireball. Nothing more, nothing less. I couldn't have fit another morsel of food into my belly because I was literally bursting at the seams. (And don't DM me saying I should eat more veggies. I usually eat pretty healthy but when I'm on vacay it is greasy foods *only*.)

Anyway! There was a light at the end of my tunnel of constipation: I had prescription laxatives at home that were to be used *only* for emergencies. Even though this was all my fault, it was still 100% considered an emergency. I was counting down the hours until I could pop one of those pills and expel the fifty pounds of trash currently chilling in my intestines. And let me tell you, these laxatives *work*. They work so well that, for at least five hours following ingestion, you need to be no more than two feet away from a toilet. You never know when the next wave will hit, and each wave is worse than the last. I actually don't know how they haven't been taken off the market yet because they literally suck every ounce of hydration and nutrients you have out of your butthole with each and every shit. I don't doubt that someone must have died by accidentally taking one too many at some point. I won't tell you the brand name because I do not condone taking these death pills, but I will share some incredible review highlights I found:

Looking for a way to embarrass yourself? Look no further!
Death would have been welcome . . .
A Grave Mistake
One too many cost me a night in the hospital
Food poisoning couldn't have been worse
AWFUL
HELL—don't recommend it!
Most pain I've experienced in my life
YOU WILL BE SICK FOR DAYS!!! YES, FOR DAYS!!
Never again!

Sounds fun, right? So anyway, I get home from vacation and pop the laxative. They're kind of like edibles in the sense that they take a few hours to work and you contemplate taking another in the interim because you feel like nothing is happening. And then out of nowhere, *shit hurricane*.

And this is where the monetary part of the story begins. Because, in true Joe Exotic style, this one laxative was a huge hit to me financially. It all started with the underwear I was wearing that afternoon, a $29 Victoria's Secret seamless thong. Didn't make it to the bathroom fast enough for the first wave. *Ruined.* So, I changed into another pair of VS underwear because I'm an idiot and must have blacked out the trauma of endless trips to the bathroom from the last time I desperately took this laxative. Ten minutes later, *ruined.* Another $29. And I wasn't being lazy or slow on my journey to the bathroom . . . these waves come on so fast that if you aren't on the toilet within three seconds, you're screwed. And listen, I know I could have washed them, but a thirty-four-year-old washing the literal shit stains out of her own underwear is a line I just will not cross. I'll save the poopy underwear for when I have a baby one day. After the second wave though, I wised up and threw on some cheap older underwear. But don't worry, I ruined a few pairs of those, too. We'll tally that up to a total of $25 more.

After a few hours, the waves started slowing and finally stopped by bedtime. I felt cleared out and back to normal with only a few underwear casualties. Ahhhh, laxative success! Except . . . it wasn't.

Fast forward to 3:00 a.m. when I was jolted awake with dripping night sweats and stomach pain from the devil himself. I raced to the bathroom, but it was too late: $19 underwear, $299 linen duvet cover and fitted sheet, and $39 mattress cover *ruined.* And *thank God* I had the mattress cover on, or else there would have been a thousand-dollar mattress casualty as well. I spent the next four hours on the toilet because I had already lost so much, and my soul couldn't bear another hit.

By 7:00 a.m., it slowed down enough that I could create some distance from the bathroom, but I was emotionally, physically, and spiritually depleted. I was so exhausted and delirious that I accidentally took my sleeping medicine instead of my probiotics that morning. I missed out on a last-minute, time-sensitive work opportunity that cost me $1,500 because I was too scared to be away from the toilet and obviously couldn't drive or function for that matter. I also missed my dentist appointment, and my dentist was really mad at me. *Fuck.* I hate disappointing Dr. Dekano. But at least I wasn't pooping my pants.

I slowly came back to life over the next twenty-four hours. The next morning I put on a pair of regular underwear again. I went on with my day. I even left the house! Bad move, Jac. Bad move. The laxative came back forty-eight hours later with a *vengeance.* While I was driving. Another $29 pair of VS undies *ruined.* And a $99 detailed car wash. I had to tell the guy at the car wash that my dog had an accident and pooped in the car. I don't even have a dog! What was I doing?! I felt so fucking sick. Why was this still happening *days* later??? How did I have this much literal shit inside my body?! Was this how I go? Death by laxative? I guess I could just lean into it. Make sure my grave says: *She Died Doing What She Loved, Pooping.*

This cycle went on for a literal week. It was a full seven days of ruining underwear, slowly feeling better, being woken up by a burning butthole, the devil ripping apart my insides, rinse and repeat. It finally went away for good one day, and I decided to celebrate by going over to my friend Alexis's house for a drink while we both did some work on our computers. As I was telling her my shit saga and totaling the monetary loss I had experienced so far, she goes, "SHUT THE FUCK UP!" and flailed her arms in the air out of emphasis. During said flail, she proceeded to knock her beer directly onto my laptop. My $1,900 thirteen-inch Macbook Pro . . . ruined.

In total, that laxative cost me $3,968 and a lifetime of shame. The underwear, sheets, and laptop I can replace. But my dignity is gone forever.

KELTIE: THE OSCAR FOR THE SHADIEST BITCH GOES TO . . . ME!

The Academy Awards are the biggest night in Hollywood. When I was a kid, I would drool, waiting for the glorious Sunday night where we all huddled around our living room TV to watch the Oscars. Once a year, from my hometown in the prairies of Canada (best known for being next door to the World's Largest Ukrainian Easter Egg), we got a peek into Hollywood glitz, glamour, and stars. Back then, we didn't have the 24-7 news cycle or social media where there's always a sneak peek at something glamorous. Oscar night was exceptional.

Fast forward about twenty-five years and I found myself working as an entertainment correspondent for one of the biggest television shows in the world. Covering Oscar night was my job. In Los Angeles, the Oscars are much more than just the award ceremony and the statues. All over the city there are parties, events, after-parties, and viewing parties, so that any stars that are not invited to the actual awards ceremony have a place to go, get dressed up for, and be seen.

There's actually a hierarchy to the whole thing. Allow me to explain this all to you. First, The Elton John Oscar party is a significant event, with the proceeds going to his foundation. It is a "viewing party," which means the stars arrive early in the afternoon at the same time they would be walking the red carpet at the Oscars if they were nominated. They walk Elton's red carpet and then sit through the whole four-hour ceremony inside, eat dinner, and then party into the wee hours of the night. The Elton John party has a broad mix of celebrities, some A-plus-list names, but mostly B and C, who didn't get invited to any more fabulous parties. However, Elton's personal Rolodex runs deep, so there is always good celeb spotting on the carpet.

And then, there's the *Vanity Fair* Oscar party. The crème de la crème of celebrities are invited to this ultra-exclusive event. The guest list is usually filled with models, actors who have actually won Oscars, music royalty, hot journalists of the moment, and Larry David. I've covered this party so many times that I would wear a gown and uncomfortable shoes in my early years and stand in the cold for ten hours happily without even a drink of water just because I was so jazzed to have such a chic assignment. In my later years though, I got brilliant! I started bringing a cooler of snacks, a small chair, a heating pad to warm my hands and feet when I got too cold at night, and various other accoutrements to make the never-ending shift more enjoyable. Like Elton's party, *Vanity Fair*'s is a viewing party, so it's a long night. The difference is that getting your photo taken in a designer gown on the *Vanity Fair* carpet is like some sort of star meter in Hollywood yelling from the top of its lungs, "Alert! Alert! This person matters."

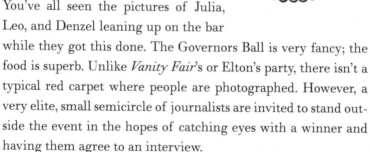

The last of the exclusive Oscar parties is the Governors Ball. The Governors Ball is right next door to the actual location of the Oscars ceremony. It's a big deal because it's where the winners of the evening come to get their Oscars engraved. You've all seen the pictures of Julia, Leo, and Denzel leaning up on the bar while they got this done. The Governors Ball is very fancy; the food is superb. Unlike *Vanity Fair*'s or Elton's party, there isn't a typical red carpet where people are photographed. However, a very elite, small semicircle of journalists are invited to stand outside the event in the hopes of catching eyes with a winner and having them agree to an interview.

My first time covering the Governors Ball was a big deal. It meant that I was the most senior correspondent the show had and that I was trusted to be around the night's big winners. In addition to being assigned to work the Governors Ball, I was also being credentialed for the official Oscars red carpet earlier in the day, in case anything happened to the show's hosts (like, if they got sick). There was a lot of pressure on me, and I spent hours making sure that every hair, jewel, and factoid was perfect. My executive producer at the time was very into fashion and very involved with my look. She wanted the show's hosts to level up their fashion game, which I loved. When I showed her my black gown with the jeweled bodice, she was giddy, saying, "You better walk the carpet in that beauty!" Since I was credentialed to go on the actual carpet and love having my picture taken in beautiful clothes, I got ready early, went to the early photo call on the carpet, and then immediately walked off the carpet back to the hotel room and waited five hours until I was needed at the Governors Ball to catch up with the winners. I was a young and hungry baby reporter, and being seen at the biggest night of the year, to me, was a significant win. I didn't break any rules, and I got my pics on *Vogue*'s website. God, I'm so pathetic.

Jump to the awards season of 2016. I worked nonstop and knew awards season would mean many sleepless nights, fifteen-hour days, and countless outfits. Instead of the last-minute scramble of finding something to wear to each of the major ceremonies, I got smart and planned all my looks for all the awards shows before the bell had even rung on New Year's Eve! I love being a showgirl and dressing up. Plus, I was starting to get enough attention in the press to use my red carpet powers for good. Being Canadian, I really wanted to support a Canadian designer on the red carpet and show off my home-country pride, so I arranged to wear this beautiful red Canadian-designer gown to whatever assignment I would get for the Oscars by promising that I would be walking the carpet and getting photographed.

The process of getting a dress is an insane fashion dance that most D-list humans have to deal with. The A-list stars have exclusive deals with couture houses for custom gowns and then also *get paid* hundreds of thousands of dollars to be spotted wearing a particular fashion label or jewelry brand. (Never feel bad for celebs when they complain about being asked about the dress; don't be fooled, that dress is paying for the mansion!) The B-list stars get to borrow designer brands from the runway but do not get paid. Further down, the C-list would be famous people going to either Elton's or *Vanity Fair*'s party and borrowing gowns from less sought-after designers. Waaaaaaaay down, on the bottom of the D list, was me, pleading to borrow a dress from an unheard-of Canadian designer with the promise that the gown would show up on some sort of Oscar fashion red carpet photo gallery somewhere on the internet.

I had recently started working with a personal publicist in hopes that they could guide my budding career and grow me from baby correspondent into the next Giuliana Rancic–type, empire running, boss babe. The publicist had secured a fantastic opportunity to partner with *Elle Canada* because I would be wearing a Canadian-designed dress. I would do a whole-day takeover with them and an article featuring my look. This entire fashion song and dance was signed, sealed, and delivered before I even knew what my assignment for the show would be, but I had been working the awards seasons for many years at this point and I knew I'd get some sort of red carpet access. If it wasn't at Elton's party, it would be *Vanity Fair*'s, and if it wasn't *Vanity Fair*, I'd at least be back at the Governors Ball like the year before. And that's precisely what happened. I was assigned to cover the Governors Ball again and was thrilled! My plan was working perfectly! I'd just do what I had done last time and walk the early carpet and then wait around till it was time to actually work. And because I had done all my fashion planning months ahead, maybe I could even use my extra time for more beauty sleep (just kidding, hosts don't sleep during awards season!). But, there was one major issue. For a reason I can't remember, I did not get an Oscars red carpet credential. I was only given a pass to stand outside the Governors Ball, the one party that was sans red carpet. My entire *Elle* magazine/Canadian star-making moment was falling apart. I was *screwed.*

Now, I have built my entire career on making impossible things possible, so I just needed a plan to get my photo taken—in the dress—at the Oscars. A lightbulb went off! There was a production assistant in our team who had similar features to mine, *and she was credentialed.* I had been the queen of fake IDs when I was seventeen years old and sneaking into Club Malibu in Edmonton every weekend. I figured, if I convinced my twin PA to let me borrow her identity for about twenty minutes at the start of the event and act like I'm supposed to be there, I just may get away with it! She very hesitantly agreed to help me out, and the plan seemingly worked perfectly. I swiped "my" security pass, rocked that red dress, and posed my heart out like I was fucking Giselle on that red carpet. By the time I got back to the hotel room (a mere twenty minutes later) to give the pass back to the PA, I was already being lauded worldwide on Getty Images as a red-dressed wonder.

The rest of the night was incredible. I went to my assignment at the Governors Ball. I did some great interviews. I got home at 2:00 a.m., googled myself for an hour or so, and then got up at 4:30 a.m. to go back to work. Everything seemed great! The dress designer was thrilled, my *Elle* magazine article was out, and I felt I was definitely on my way to superstardom.

Then I got caught.

I got called into the office of one of the senior producers, Bonnie Tiegel. Bonnie passed away a few years after this story, but she was a freaking legend in Hollywood. This woman was loud, fiery, and had almost every A-list star's personal cell phone number in her Rolodex. (Bonnie had been a mentor and a friend to me when I was first starting out. We used to meet in the parking lot at 3:45 a.m., me for my 4:15 a.m. news hit, and her because she always got into the office at 4:30 a.m., before everyone else.) Bonnie was livid. She had seen my red carpet photos and had explicitly known that I was not credentialed for that specific security clearance. She had worked backward and uncovered my entire evil genius plan. I had been so laser-focused on not screwing over the dress designer and blinded by the shine of an *Elle* feature that I hadn't stopped to think that perhaps lying and breaking the rules at the freaking Oscars maybe wasn't the most professional way to go. Looking back on this, I'm shocked that I didn't get fired. I did get in a lot of trouble, *and* I got the PA in a lot of trouble. Then again, as a reporter, you're often celebrated for getting secret scoops or sneaking backstage at the Super Bowl to get your soundbite with Beyoncé. So eventually, everyone on staff moved on to the next big thing.

I was, however, never asked to cover the Governors Ball or be anywhere around the actual Oscars red carpet ever again. In the years following my stolen identity incident, I was demoted to being a *Vanity Fair* girl. To be honest, the whole situation was super stressful, and after that, I stopped trying so hard to be a star. I realized how pathetic my desperation and thirst were; when I walked out of Bonnie's office with my tail between my legs, I realized that I was actually the most uncool because I was trying so hard to be cool. I had to get honest with myself that if I was going to get the level of success that I wanted from my career, it would be because of hard work, dedication, loyalty, and reputation, not some stupid borrowed dress. I stopped dressing up for the Oscars that year, and for the next three years, I simply wore the same ASOS suit with a stolen tuxedo tie from my husband and secondhand Prada loafers. It was way more comfortable and definitely easier on my heart to know I wasn't making a promise I couldn't keep. And let's be honest, the only person who was excited to see me in some Oscars fashion gallery was me. Harsh but true.

BECCA: MY INFLUENCER LIFE

I am thirty-five years old and I have a new addiction: TikTok. I'm embarrassed. I'm ashamed. I'm all the terrible things.

I rejected TikTok in the beginning because all I saw were crop top–wearing preteens doing body rolls and sticking their tongues out. No disrespect, but that content brings me zero joy, for two reasons. First, it makes me feel elderly, and second, I resent anyone who gets rich and famous from having a limited skillset. Yes, I'm bitter.

So, after playing around on the app during the pandemic and deciding I was just too old to understand its appeal, I deleted it and moved on with my heavy *ahem* cheugy Instagram use.

But then, something wonderful/horrible happened: Rob, a famous Hollywood stylist who I follow on Instagram, started putting his "favorite TikToks of the week" up on his stories every Friday. That motherfucker!!! Suddenly I was seeing animals doing incredible things with hilarious voiceovers and husbands taking out the garbage while doing stripteases to turn their wives on. I found myself smiling and giggling and *looking forward to Fridays*! FUUUUUCKKKKK! But still every other day of the week—I convinced myself that TikTok was super lame and not for me. I mean, Rob must be spending all his time sorting through the bullshit dance videos on TikTok to find these diamonds amongst the rhinestones, right?

I went on like this for a while, limiting my TikTok exposure to just Fridays, until one dark, gloomy day in Texas when I did the unthinkable. I reinstalled my TikTok app and signed back into my account! I scrolled and scrolled and scrolled and . . . *oh, my sweet baby Jesus*, there were *so many* videos that tickled my fancy. There was the tiny dog who attacked its owner, whose only retort was to flip him the middle finger! Or the burly construction worker who brought his tiny, obsessed, raccoon pet to work with him (to the soundtrack from a romantic eighties movie, natch!), or the dogs who ran/vaulted/jumped/climbed over fences and other obstacles (to Michael Scott screaming "parkour" in the background!). I had hit the mother lode! And I found myself feeling a strange, new feeling . . . could it be pure unabashed joy?! *Yes*, yes it was!

I'm happy to report that while I rarely participate in the content creation of the app, I cannot deny any longer that I am a loyal-as-fuck viewer. I'm sorry to everyone I've been lying to about hating this platform and hoping it would go away or get banned from the United States or whatever people have been threatening. The truth is . . . I would be devastated.

JAC: WANDER-*BUST*

I pride myself on being an *excellent* traveler. In fact, it's one of my biggest and best talents in life, and I make sure to let everyone know it. Any time I plan a trip to a new city, I spend hours and hours and hours researching the very best way to spend my time. I always try to immerse myself in the food, drinks, sights, sounds, culture, and every little detail of each new city I visit, and vehemently refuse to do anything "touristy." I would rather be caught dead than take a photo holding the Leaning Tower of Pisa or pose in front of Big Ben. Instead, I try to find unconventional, offbeat experiences in every new city, which is why I am *obsessed* with *Atlas Obscura.* Per its website, *Atlas Obscura* is "an online magazine and travel company that catalogs unusual and obscure travel destinations via user-generated content." Basically, *Atlas Obscura* shows you interesting, curious experiences all over the world that you'd *never* find on your own. And a bonus is that a lot of it is super weird and creepy! For example, instead of seeing the Eiffel Tower in Paris, *Atlas Obscura* directs you to the Catacombes de Paris, the remnants of the Paris guillotine, and "In the Dark," a restaurant where you dine in complete darkness. Cool shit if you ask me.

So, I started using *Atlas Obscura* for all of my trips, and it wouldn't be any different on my trip to Portugal in 2019 with my fiancé, Jared. While having our 578th glass of delicious dollar Vinho Verde on our first of two nights in Lisbon, Jared and I started browsing *Atlas Obscura* for some unique destinations we could see in between eating and drinking our way through the city. I typed "Lisbon" in the search bar and started browsing. I scrolled past a dilapidated monastery, a 400-year-old candle shop, and a seashell gallery, and *boom*, I locked eyes with the image of a man's decapitated head in a jar. Yes, you heard me right. A real human's head. In a jar. The link beneath this shocking image stated:

PRESERVED HEAD OF DIOGO ALVES. An Early Portuguese Serial Killer's Head Is Alarmingly Well Preserved In A Jar At The University Of Lisbon.

And when they say "alarmingly" well preserved, they truly do mean it. It was *so* well preserved that it looked fake, like it should be displayed in Madame Tussauds next to Ariana Grande or something. They pickled this fucker's head like Bloody Mary accoutrements, and it has really held up over the years (which is a good life hack to know, I guess?). This was legit the weirdest shit I had ever come across on *Atlas Obscura*, and it was *so* on brand for me! Searching through a new town on the hunt for a serial killer's pickled head?? Count. Me. In.

Before we jump into my adventure, I wanted to give a little summary about this Diogo Alves character. During the 1830s, this piece of shit would stand on a 200-foot-high aqueduct, rob farmers as they passed, and push them to their death! After he got bored of that, he started just straight up robbing and killing people in their homes. He killed seventy people total. He was Portugal's first known serial killer and was apparently the last person in the country to be executed via hanging.

So, first things first. I obviously had to study Diogo's glorious head. To quote from the article, "[The head] is yellow, peaceful looking, and somewhat akin to a potato." The first thing I noticed was the fact that his head was decapitated very cleanly right under the chin. It was just like . . . chilling at the bottom of the jar, and it fit quite perfectly in there (file under #oddlysatisfying). He looked straight up *comfy* in there. His expression was cool, calm, and collected. Diogo had a full, thick head of light red hair, which was nicely coiffed and floating around a bit in the pickling substance. Diogo's eyes were open, but his lids were slightly closed. Kind of like he was staring off into the abyss having some sort of existential crisis, or like he was dreading having to apologize to his girlfriend later that night for playing video games on their anniversary. His eyes were kind of close together, and he didn't seem to have visible eyebrows. His skin was fucking impeccable, not a single wrinkle or blemish in sight. He seemed to have some day-old scruff, which he must have cleaned up recently before he was decapitated (gotta look good even in death, my dude). The quality of his head was pristine. No decomp, no skin flapping off, no visible abrasions. He honestly looked . . . alive. And I was thinking more of a mason jar when I read the "head in a jar" description, but he was chillin' in what looked like a glass vase they'd give you for the cheap option at 1-800-FLOWERS. And whatever liquid Diogo was floating in was amber in color, which made him look like he was sepia toned, like those touristy old-timey cowboy photos you'd take at Knott's Berry Farm.

Upon further examination of the photo of Diogo Alves, there was something about him that felt . . . I dunno . . . familiar to me? I was scratching my own head while studying Diogo's head, trying to put my finger on it. It was on the tip of my tongue, but, ugh, I couldn't figure it out. In a moment of frustration, I glanced up to Jared, and that's when it hit me. *Diogo Alves was Jared's fucking twin.* I'm not kidding, look for yourself. Google "Diogo

Alves head" and "Jared Monaco" and tell me you *don't* see a striking resemblance. Was Jared a Portuguese serial killer in his past life? Did the universe bring us to this very moment? Would Jared touching Diogo change the course of history forever? There was only one way to find out. *We had to find the head.*

According to the article on *Atlas Obscura*, the head was sitting in the anatomical theater at the University of Lisbon's Faculty of Medicine, which was open to the public. And I'm sure this comes as no surprise, but neither Jared nor I knew a word of

Portuguese. But we figured between the straightforward directions and a picture of the head to show anyone for reference, locating the jar would be a piece of cake, and we'd make it out with a great Instagram pic in time for brunch. Oh, Jac. You silly little fool.

We parked in the University of Lisbon parking lot, made our way into the building, and found the anatomical theater in a few minutes. Damn, that was easy! I grabbed the handle to swing the door open, and . . . it was locked. So we started wandering the halls asking anyone we passed if they knew where the head was. *And no one knew what we were talking about.* We even showed them the picture! Hellooooo???? Was I being Punk'd? Where the hell was Ashton?! I'm sorry, but if the pickled head of the most notorious serial killer of my country was just chilling on a shelf in *my* workplace, I could've led you there in no time. I'd even get keychains made with mini Diogo jarred heads to give out as souvenirs. So, after a handful of poor clueless professors, we finally found a receptionist who was familiar with Diogo. Through a translator app, she told us the head was in the building next door. Ahhh yes, a classic mix-up!

We made our way next door and things immediately felt, I don't know . . . chaotic? We kept asking people about Diogo and kept getting directed to different eerie corners of the building, and every room was stranger than the last. We saw some weird shit on our hunt including but not limited to: abandoned classrooms, busy lecture halls, what looked like top-secret meetings, people whispering, people screaming, dilapidated basements, barren rooftops, lost-and-founds, some kind of experiments??? *Bone saws??* The vibe was . . . off. It felt like we shouldn't be allowed to be there, but we walked right through an open public entrance, so I guess we were?

We were about to hit hour five of our search for Diogo when my stomach started rumbling, and I needed a little snackie-poo for sustenance on our excursion. I spotted a vending machine in the distance, and as I made my way out into another new, intriguing hallway, it hit me. Scrubs, wheelchairs, stethoscopes, heart monitors, and stretchers slowly began to fill my view. Are we in a . . . hospital????? Have I been so hyperfocused on the hunt for this stupid pickled head that I failed to realize we had been aimlessly wandering around a Portuguese hospital for half a day?!

As this embarrassing realization overcomes me, a nurse at the receptionist desk calls us over, obviously assuming we were walk-in patients. I froze. I was at a crossroads. Do I ask her about Diogo or succumb to my failure and bail? I bravely decided to channel my inner Robert Frost and took the road less traveled to the pickled head. What's the harm in asking *one* more person? I valiantly held up the picture of Diogo and asked if she knew anything about him. She didn't say anything, but she glanced at my phone super quick, looked at Jared, and wrote something down on a notepad. She politely smiled, nodded her head, and before we knew it, we were being escorted into a room down the hall where we assumed Diogo was on display.

The nurse left and closed the door as we sat down, so we just started searching every inch of this room for the head to no avail. We waited in that little room for what felt like hours, hoping a medical historian would bust through the door like a knight in shining armor with Diogo's decapitated head in his arm like some kind of medieval prize. Finally . . . the doorknob turned, we held our breath, and to our surprise, a doctor walked in. He was *not* carrying the head, BTW. He spoke a *little* bit of English. While looking straight at Jared, he said that the nurse at the reception desk had seen a photo of a man with a bloated face. *Oh my God*, the doctor thinks Jared is Diogo! BAHAHA I knew it! They *are* twins. As the doctor started to take Jared's blood pressure without warning, poor Jared had to frantically try to explain to him that the man in the photo was the pickled head of a Portuguese serial killer from the 1800s, *not* him. But like I said, the doctor spoke very little English, so he just kept on taking Jared's vitals while I was trying not to have a laughing attack in the corner of the room (I have laughing attacks when I'm nervous, FYI). A few minutes into this mess, a nurse entered the room and we broke down and told her everything. The history of Diogo, the endless search for the head in a jar, accidentally ending up in the hospital, how Jared actually isn't Diogo, everything. As incredible as the story was, we were so freakin' embarrassed! She translated our disaster of a day to the doctor, and they just burst out laughing. She brought up the picture of Diogo and held it next to Jared's head, comparing the similarities between the two with the doctor. When she finally caught her breath, she explained to us that she knew exactly who Diogo was and that his head was just taken on a traveling tour around Portugal. Excuse me? He's on *tour*? *Like a goddamn rockstar???* Just. My. Luck. The doctor and nurse excused themselves for a few minutes before coming back and letting us go.

By the time we exited the waiting room, the secret was out. All the health care workers on the floor knew. As we took the most mortifying walk of shame out of the hallway of that hospital wing, all eyes were on us. Everyone was laughing, whispering, or asking about Diogo. We bolted out of there like two dogs with our tails between our legs and drowned out the pain with a few bottles of wine that night. We had officially wasted 75% of our time in Lisbon looking for that goddamn head. And I'm sure our photos are displayed on the wall somewhere on that floor of the hospital with the note WATCH OUT FOR DUMB AMERICANS. Looking back, by trying *so* hard to not be a stupid tourist, I ended up being the stupidest tourist of all time. Fuck.

KELTIE: AU REVOIR, CLOONEY!

Anyone who travels for work will tell you that you get to go *everywhere*, but you get to see and experience *nothing*. While out on assignment, it was infrequent for me to get a night off and, even if I did, I'd usually be so overworked and tired from the jet lag that I couldn't even force myself to go out and explore or be social. However, there was one work destination that was the exception: France. Being alone in France just felt different than other work trips. My daydreamer tendencies made me believe that behind each tiny cobblestone lane was the possibility of the next great vintage store or life-changing cheese plate or perfect glass of wine. Somehow, I always pulled my sleep-deprived self out of my hotel to explore.

It was the Cannes Film Festival that brought me to France. Cannes is—by far—the most glamorous and elite movie event in the world. Even if you've never seen a movie that screened at the festival, you've probably had your jaw drop seeing the fantasy photos of couture gowns gliding up the famous red-sided stairs. The red carpet is oversized and even more elegant than the Oscars. Cannes is *the* place to be seen, so A-listers flock yearly to the tiny French town to promote their projects, and I was fortunate to be on assignment there for a few days interviewing those A-listers.

On one of those beyond perfect summer evenings that only happen in Cannes, a couple of fellow TV host friends in town mentioned that they were using their night off to go and have a cocktail . . . and I actually said "Oui!" and decided to tag along. My friends and I got dressed up and grabbed a taxi (from our waaaay less desirable hotel) and arrived at the world-famous Hôtel du Cap-Eden-Roc. Hôtel du Cap is quite possibly the most beautiful hotel in the world. It looks like a palace. It's made entirely of stone and, on the backside of the hotel, there's a superwide, epic staircase that looks like it came right out of the "midnight-glass-slipper-left-on-the-staircase" scene in *Cinderella.* At the bottom of the stairs, the walkway continues down a wide, tree-lined path right to the crashing waves of the ocean. I mean, it's fancy as fuck.

We were trying to appear cool enough to be staying there and headed toward the bar on the main level. Inside, the hotel looks a lot like the fake Kensington Palace that they show on *The Crown.* It has that unique mix of everything being super old, but it's so well taken care of that it feels brand new. Everywhere you turn, there's a tiny piece of art or a little floral detail that makes the place so special. We ordered our incredibly overpriced glasses of wine and walked outside to a small patio near the famous staircase to sit, people watch, and just feel fabulous.

It was surprisingly empty for being the most critical hotel at the Cannes Film Festival. But, that was indeed the calm before the storm. Our first little brush with fame was running into celeb-fav makeup artist Charlotte Tilbury. She was the woman behind Amal Clooney's famous wedding day glam perfection, and I had interviewed her a couple of times. (She's also the maker of a lipstick called "bitch perfect," which I consider my signature lip.) This Charlotte sighting should've been an indicator that the Clooneys could be near, but I didn't think much of it. She has so many A-list clients that you just expect her to be around during these types of weeks.

Once we finished our wine, my mighty trio of journalist friends and I decided to take a walk around the property. We descended the famous staircases, posed for Instagram photos (of course), and then spied a building down by the water with two huge security guards standing outside the front door. Without even discussion, one of my friends walked over to them, hand extended, saying, "Hey man, good to see you." The guards simply uncrossed their arms and ushered us into this beautiful ocean-side restaurant. I can't remember if he said it to me at the time or if I just thought it in my head, but I'm almost positive that the same friend turned to me and said, "See, if you just act like you belong, they let you in anywhere."

When we got inside, we walked down some glass stairs to the main level. It was the most beautiful space I've ever seen— idyllic white railings, a bar on the left, and a glass floor. There were huge doors that led out to a glass terrace, and when you looked right over the edge, you were on top of the ocean. All you could hear was the melodic sound of the waves crashing on the rocks. It was truly spectacular. There was a giant bar filled with seafood on ice and waiters walking around passing hors d'oeuvres like they would at a wedding. And when they asked us our drink orders and brought our drinks, there was nary a bill in sight. At some point, I figured out that this was some sort of private party, but it was the most extraordinary party I'd ever been to, so I was not planning on leaving.

We made small talk with each other, enjoyed the ocean view for a few minutes, and then suddenly, there was a scurry of activity to our left. A large entourage was making its way inside, and that sweet smell of fame changed the air in the room. Everyone's eyes darted toward whatever famous person was in the middle of the crowd. That famous person turned out to be *one of the most famous people on the planet*, George Clooney, whom I had literally just interviewed three hours before as a part of the press junket for his movie. (As an interviewer, you do see a lot of stars at formal press events, but rarely are you exposed to them in the wild.)

George was dazzling. I mean, he is so handsome in real life that you can't even understand it. It's unfair! He just keeps getting more dapper as the years go on. He will probably someday star in *Oceans 72* and still be cute! George flashed his megawatt smile at everyone in the room and started making the rounds, saying hi to all the small groups of people. Eventually, George Clooney came upon the three of us, the uninvited guests. He shook my friend's hand! He gave me a French double-cheek air kiss! He said, "Hey, great to see you!" as if we were long-lost best friends reunited after a lengthy separation! He spent twenty-five seconds of his George Clooney life small talking and charming us so much that I thought, *Well, you know what? I wasn't invited, but we have a friendship I was not aware of; I think I'm going to grab another drink, one of those jumbo shrimp, and settle in for a long, fun night. I'll probably be swapping lipstick stories with Amal by the end of the evening!*

As Batman was whisked away to hang with other party-goers, our trio was approached by his longtime publicist . . . who was not quite as thrilled to see us. In that lovely way that all Hollywood publicists can tell you no and break your heart—all while flashing their warmest smile—we heard the dreaded words, "So . . . yeah you guys have got to go, you can't be here." There would be no passing go, there would be no second drink, there would be no giant shrimp cocktail. The gig was up. We had accidentally crashed two-time Academy Award–winning George Clooney's private party, and for us, the party was over. It didn't matter how much we both loved our Nespresso machine; we had nothing in common. He was a star, and I was simply a cog in the publicity machine that fed his fame. We put our drink glasses down on the bar, hung our heads, and headed up the glass staircase away from the party and back into our existence as mere uncool normie mortals.

The moral of the story is that faking it till you make it is a real thing. If you hold your head high and act like you're supposed to be in a room (that you are truly not meant to be in), for the most part, you'll get by. Unless it's George Clooney's party and he wants to get wild and take his Casamigos shots in private and you are a member of the press. The second moral of the story is that George Clooney is the best fucking actor on the planet. I mean, please give this man another Oscar for this Cannes party performance! The emotion! The goosebumps! The truth in his eyes portraying his excitement and happiness of seeing me at his party when I wasn't even invited. It was George

Clooney's best role. To be honest, I have judged each of his movies against this personal "scene" we shared in France and none of his roles come even close to this level of acting. So, bravo Georgie! And sorry I crashed your party!

P.S. You missed out, because when I take Casamigos shots, I'm a really fun time.

BECCA: SUNNY-SIDE UP . . . WITH A SIDE OF MORTIFICATION

I consider this story one of my top three most embarrassing experiences in my life. And, yes, you might have heard it before on the podcast many moons ago, but, hey, what could be braver than having it printed in thousands of books for anyone to read at leisure? So here ya go . . .

The year was 2014 and I had just started dating my now-husband, Zach. We were blissfully in that "new relationship" phase where we still coexisted like some strange, beautiful aliens who never pooped, only had wonderful breath, and were completely hairless and smooth from head-to-toe like a baby seal—well, at least I was.

I was working on *Glee* at the time, which meant long, fifteen-hour days of singing and dancing in a cheerleading uniform complete with . . . polyester bloomers! You can imagine how moist things got down there. I have always required a very clean and dry ecosystem in my nether regions to perform at my best, so I made sure to keep baby wipes and extra thongs handy to avoid ever having to deal with a sweaty crotch or, worse, bacterial vaginosis.

One day I was sitting upstairs in my apartment waiting for Zach to come back from an errand (no doubt ready to jump his bones, new relationship and all) when he walks through my front door and casually says, "I found this in the parking garage . . . on the ground by the elevator . . . I think it's yours?" and throws me a tiny (slightly crunchy?) wisp of lace. I instantly recognized it as a $22 Hanky Panky thong. MY. $22. Hanky. Panky. Thong. I wanted to die.

Thankfully, he had the decency to be nonchalant about it and just tossed it and walked away, because what I feared most was the other side of that lacy pocket. So, when he was finally out of the room, I frantically flipped the underwear inside-out and saw . . . it. The thing that should remain a mystery to all men forever: a dried-up, white, flaky mess that looks like the inside of a pan after cooking egg whites. My body went cold; I avoided eye contact for several hours.

Eventually, when our infatuation spell was broken (most likely after one of us accidentally farted in front of the other) we were able to move past this tragedy and even laugh about it. As I had suspected/feared all these months, the now infamous HP thong had indeed been laying crotch up—nay, *sunny-side up*—in that parking garage for all to see. Yup. And, it had definitely been the first time he had seen such a thing. I would love to be able to say that I gave him an education on female discharge that day, or that we acted like mature adults, but we both kinda just agreed that an abandoned, snail-trail-encrusted thong is one of the most disgusting things ever seen by the human eye.

A TALL TAIL

My dad has always joked about this, and I guess there's not much I can do as it's been there since I was a baby, but I have a tail. Okay, not actually a *tail*-tail, as in, like it wags or has a curly end like a pig. It's probably more of a very large skin tag. Either way, there is something very odd near my butthole. It doesn't really bother me most days, because it just sort of hangs there, and it doesn't hurt because it's just skin. Still, I feel weird when I think about my butthole, or rather, anyone seeing my butthole, because it's not perfect. No one's ever brought it up, and a new partner usually doesn't see it, or is too busy with other things to really notice it's there. It's one of those things that really doesn't affect my day-to-day life, but I would definitely like to have it removed at some point. My parents are really the only ones that make a lot of jokes about it at this point, and I'm an adult so I can take it. However, I've been with the same guy for five years. He's never brought it up either, but I do remember one time, when we were first hooking up, he kind of grazed it. Later, when I was looking something up on his phone, I noticed he had a tab open and had been googling "butthole skin tag." So embarrassing. I would like to have a really nice, normal, tail-free butthole. A girl can dream.

THIS DATE SUCKS

It was the second date with a high school boyfriend of mine. We went to a movie and had our fill of soda, popcorn, Milk Duds, and Mike and Ikes. By the end of the movie it had all caught up with me, and I had to use the ladies' room. While my date politely waited outside in the lobby, I went into a stall to do number one and number two, and that's when it happened. Somehow, leaning down to flush the toilet, I watched in slow motion as my brand new cell phone did a perfect dive right into the bowl. I panicked. I was absolutely horrified. It immediately went black and wouldn't turn back on. I didn't know what to do. I was super devastated because I knew my parents would be so pissed, having just handed it to me a few weeks before, alongside a whole lecture about responsibility and taking care of nice things. Well, this is why I can't have nice things! I scrambled to try to figure out what to do, but I also knew my boyfriend would probably get weirded out if I stayed in the stall forever. I tried running the phone under the hand dryer, and this woman gave me a look so I hightailed it back to the lobby, holding that nasty phone in my hand. I told my boyfriend that I'd dropped the phone in the sink when I was washing my hands, and that it wouldn't turn on. Before I could stop him, this boy grabbed the phone *and started sucking the water out of it. My poop and pee water.* I honestly stared at him in disgust, while he slurped away at that phone. Here I was, hoping to get my first real kiss, and that boy had just . . . I still cringe when I think about it. I couldn't tell him. I couldn't tell anyone.

SHITTY KITTY

I am lactose intolerant (you can already guess where this is headed), but that doesn't keep me down. I still eat ice cream and cheese even though I know I will end up paying a price for it. One night, I'd smoked a little too much and was like, "You know what sounds great right now? A big old Dairy Queen blizzard." So, I went out, got a blizzard, and was living my best life until about two in the morning when all that lactose caught up with me and things started to go south.

I was getting up multiple times every hour, just sitting on the toilet, feeling my life flash before my very eyes. I felt like I was dying. It was like the kind of bathroom experience in which you just want to get in the shower because you can't even wipe anymore. What's worse, my boyfriend was sleeping in the next room, so I was also trying my hardest not to let him see me like this. Finally, after the worst night of sleep, I woke up for the final show. My boyfriend was not in bed with me then, and we only had one bathroom, so I prayed and prayed that he'd left for work already. No dice. Of course he hadn't. He was in that bathroom, taking his dear sweet time. I was sweating, shaking, losing my will to live, knocking on the door, trying to get him to hurry up. Pleading with him to get out because I'm about to poop my pants, only to find out he's pooping in there and won't be done in the foreseeable future. I kicked the bathroom door, wobbled away and tried to take stock of my options. My pants, or outside. I didn't want to shit my pants because that would be messy and hard to clean up before he came out. I realized I can't shit outside either because what would happen if one of my neighbors saw me going full *Bridesmaids* in my own yard?

Desperation is the mother of invention, and I was desperate. I looked around frantically trying to figure out where the hell I was going to relieve myself, and out of the corner of my eye, I spied our cat's litter box. I am not proud of what came next. Moral of the story is if you don't want to shit in your yard, and you don't want to shit in your pants, and your boyfriend is currently occupying your only bathroom, you can use the last best option and shit in your cat's litter box.

VAGINA FLYTRAP

In my twenties I experienced a situation so bizarre that I have never had the guts to admit it to anyone. One morning, I woke up to feeling rather itchy down there. The feeling was like when there's hair in your underwear and you have to get it out, not because it's painful, but because it is just irritating enough to keep you wildly distracted. After a quick check—no hair—I just couldn't figure out what was going on. I hadn't been hooking up with anyone so that wasn't the source, and I knew I didn't have any infections. Upon deeper inspection (like, very deep), I discovered the source of my strange discomfort. A dead fly. There was a dead fly in my vagina. Why and how the fuck did it get up there? I had no idea. I still have no idea. It would have had to have been alive to crawl up so far. I think that thing was trying to get past my cervix. I was horrified. But also kind of impressed. So that's my dirty little secret—my vagina was once a Venus flytrap.

UR-INE TROUBLE

When I was seventeen, I decided I wanted to look fly as hell for the school dance, which meant I needed a tan. I made my first appointment at a local salon for a spray. At first, the lady who worked there tried to convince me to go fully orange. After talking her down a few shades, we found a good level of sun-kissed bronze. We settled on the "cocktail" approach, meaning I would start with a few minutes lying in a tanning booth and then get my spray on after. Having never experienced a tanning bed before, I was so relaxed and warm I almost fell asleep. After several minutes of absolute bliss (seriously, those things are dangerous!) I got out to head into phase two. Now, I'd seen the havoc a bad spray tan could wreak on friends of mine, so I'd taken all the precautions. I didn't want to end up with weird coverage, or funny marks because it hadn't settled evenly, or, god forbid, strange patterns on my face. It was going to look great. Or so I thought. I stood in the chamber to get spray tanned, goggles on, ready to go. The automated voiced counted down from three and when the mist hit me it was so fucking cold! It was the exact opposite of the relaxing tanning bed I was just in and shocked me so much that I peed myself in the booth. The pee kept running down my leg even as I tried to move into the correct postures in order to be evenly sprayed. It was like a scene from a bad movie. Me, just absolutely cringing as warm, tan pee puddled around my feet. I tried to clean it up as best I could, and I ran out of there as fast as possible! I didn't make eye contact with anyone in the lobby. The next day, after the tan fully developed, I had these awkward white streaks down one of my legs from where the spray tan wouldn't stick to the pee. Since that day, I've always peed *before* spray tans, even if I don't have to go. Lesson learned!

"

My ex thought he could make me squirt, but I really just peed.

"

SEX-MERGENCY

I went to a party, and by the time I got there my crush was already sloppy drunk. This party was so insane, it reminded me of a scene out of a movie. There were marketing promoters everywhere, passing out all kinds of things from condoms to little vibrating sex toy balls. After my crush passed out, I decided, since the night was still young, to go to another party with an old friend who happened to be in town. Much to my surprise, when I got there, I met the hottest nerdy guy that I have ever seen. He was visiting family for the holidays, we ended up really hitting it off, and I brought him back to my apartment. Turns out, the hot nerdy guy was a freak. In the best way. He was doing things to me that I didn't even know were possible! Then, I remembered that little vibrating sex toy ball from the first party. Hoping to help spice things up even more, I busted it out and we gave it a whirl. Now this was when things really started to get exciting.

Once we were done, I went to take the ball out, but I couldn't find it. After about ten minutes of frantically searching my vagina unsuccessfully, I started to freak out a little bit. Hot nerdy guy said he would give it a try. So there I lay on my bed with my feet up, the overhead lights shining down on me, and hot nerdy guy fishing around for this damn *vibrating* ball. Worst role-play of my life. There is no such thing as a "sexy pap-smear fantasy." After several tries, no dice. Or ball. Fuck my life. We decided to call an Uber (because we were still a little tipsy, and also an ambulance felt just too dramatic) to take me to the emergency room. Yep, that's right. I ended up in the ER to get the ball removed. When the doctor came in, I think we both knew it was the most awkward situation ever. But get this—hot nerdy guy stayed the whole night in the waiting room for me. Cute, I know. By the time we got back to my place, the sun was shining. We said our goodbyes, and I prayed to the good Lord that I would never have to see him again. I was so humiliated. I swore I'd never tell a soul.

Well, a couple weeks later I was visiting my parents, in peak post-holiday relaxation mode. My dad, who is the sweetest, kindest, most adoring dad, handed me an open invoice and said, "Don't worry, I took care of it, and I won't say anything to your mother." Yep, you guessed it. It was the invoice from my ER visit. I wanted to vanish on the spot. The description for the reason for the visit read, "Emergency physician exam. Pelvic CT. Removal of foreign bodies." Oh my god. Kill me now. We've never spoken about it again.

I'M TWENTY-FOUR YEARS OLD AND STILL SLEEP WITH MY BABY BLANKETS . . .

PEE-GASM

Once upon a time, I decided to surprise my boyfriend and let him come in my mouth. We'd had a great time, and there we were, in position, and it happened. Except, something didn't feel right. In fact, something felt completely wrong. Because he didn't come. He peed. It was pee. He was peeing in my mouth. I was so shocked, and he was so embarrassed that he almost ran out of my house naked. To make matters worse, I opened my mouth (because, you know, shock), and the pee ran out and down my body and soaked the couch. Neither of us has ever brought it up again, because who would, but now I live in fear of the accidental golden shower.

HOT GIRL BUMMER

August 2019. I was having a real "hot girl summer" in the best of ways. I was having an absolute blast and being quite irresponsible, if I'm being totally honest. Tons of great sex, over-the-top experimentation, and not much in the way of protection. One not-so-sweet day toward the end of the summer I discovered a rash near my hoo-ha. I thought to myself, *This is it. I've royally fucked up.* The worst part about my itchy vajayjay was that I didn't even know where to start with contacting all my summer lovers to tell them to get tested. My only hope was that a doctor could tell me how long I had had the rash and that would help me narrow down my very long list. I googled ferociously, hoping it would somehow reveal to me that it wasn't herpes. I studied pictures of the various common rashes (this is the best form of birth control ever) until the ones of "genital warts" were seared into my brain, and I had a strange new obsession with my own discharge. I was in a full-blown panic. Whatever was happening down there had all the markings of an STD, and after a few more days of worrying, it had started to itch.

I put off testing for about a week because I was just so ashamed and embarrassed. Finally, I couldn't take the itching anymore so I scheduled an appointment, and off to the doctor I went. As if the shame of an entire waiting room of people hearing me say out loud "I'd like to get tested for STDs" wasn't bad enough, when they asked which ones I answered meekly, "All of them." I went into the exam room, put on the gown, scooted down until I felt like I might fall off the table, and put my feet in the stirrups. The nurse swabbed me, took my blood, and then took a look at the rash. "It doesn't really look like an STD rash. We'll prescribe you some medicated powder to help, though." Well, a few days later, all my test results came back—on the phone the nurse gave me the good news. While relieved, I was genuinely shocked. I asked, "Are you sure? It's not syphilis or anything like that?" Of course, here's where it gets really good. "No, all your tests came back negative. It appears to just be some chafing."

The fabric of my pants, plus my lack of a thigh gap, in addition to the sweat from the summer heat had caused chafing that had quite literally rubbed me raw. Yup, that's right. Homegirl now has medically documented thick thighs. To this day, I have not decided which would have been less embarrassing.

WHAT WOULD GWYNETH DO?

I'm about to give Gwyneth Paltrow a run for her money. My story happened years before Goop explained the proper way to insert a hunk of jade, known as a yoni egg, into your lady bits. Did you know that "yoni" is the Sanskrit word for source, or womb? It sort of means a sacred place. Before articles about "the benefits of sticking stuff up your vag" were a thing, let's just say,

I had my own sort of encounter involving an egg, my yoni, and some less than sacred happenings.

My boyfriend and I had been together for a long time, and I was looking for ways to spice things up. I decided to bring some toys into the mix. Not the jade or crystal eggs of lore, or even anything flirty and sexy, but rather, a cheap vibrating plastic thing I'd had for a few years that happened to be shaped like an egg. We turned the thing on, in it went, and we started to go at it again. It was nice and vibey, and I was starting to relax and enjoy myself. As things got hot and heavy, naturally, it came time to remove the egg so we could have sex. Down goes the boyfriend. He pulls on the plastic-y string that was supposed to make it easy to remove the egg, and instead, it pops right off. All string, no egg. I watched that poor man's face cycle through about a million different emotions. First shock, then disbelief, and then abject horror. I burst out laughing. He tells me not to panic as, egg still buzzing away down there inside me, he throws me into a spread eagle, trying desperately to save the situation. He starts clawing away at my "yoni" to try and get it out. The problem was, I was all lubed up, and laughing, and he only succeeded in pushing it further and further out of reach. As this poor man is about to burst into tears, I had a wild idea. What, after all, are wombs for? I told him not to worry as I sat back, relaxed, and decided to try and push that stupid vibrating egg right out of my own, now slightly traumatized, hole. To both of our surprise, about three minutes later, I, er, gave birth. We both sort of stared at it in awe for a few minutes, wondering how this little piece of plastic could have caused quite so much panic. Not to worry though. Both mother and father are well, having reasonably recovered from the embarrassment.

When I was younger, maybe around age eight, I used to save my boogers in a jar in my bedroom.

GOING FOR GOLD

On my twenty-first birthday, I went to Vegas with a small group of girls. On day one of the trip we accidentally partied with a very well-known Olympian and some of his friends. There was a large group of us gambling. Like I said, my friends and I were in our early twenties, aka poor, but the Olympian and his friends were not poor. They were gambling with thousands of dollars. I thought it would be a good idea to slip a few chips in the pocket of my jeans. Harmless, right? On day two I had sex with that very well hung, very famous Olympian. The sexy time first happened in the shower. As I was ripping off my jeans, the stolen casino chips went bouncing around the huge fucking bathroom. He pretended not to notice, and we continued fucking. Mortifying, but cool. BTW: He deserves all those gold medals.

WHAT'S THE BUZZ?

I consider myself a pretty conservative lady and a strong Christian woman, but I am married and I like to have sex with my husband! A few years ago, my hubby and I went on a little getaway for our anniversary. It was his job to pack the "bow chicka wow wow supplies," and boy did he deliver. We had a great time and celebrated our anniversary with plenty of orgasms. Unbeknownst to me, he didn't unpack them after we had gotten home. At this time, our oldest son was in elementary school, and he was headed to church camp. He didn't have his own duffle bag, so I grabbed his dad's. Somehow, when I was packing him up for camp, I didn't notice that our little bullet vibrator was still in the bag!

My mother-in-law, who is even more conservative than I am,

was a counselor at this camp and was driving my kids home. In a spate of bad luck, her truck broke down about two hours away from home, and she called me to come help. I packed up my truck, grabbed my youngest, and headed off to go rescue them. In addition to my own kids, my mother-in-law also happened to be carting home from camp two of my teenaged cousins who'd volunteered to help with the session. We all piled into my car for the drive home. Keep in mind, there are now seven people stuffed into a six-seat truck. My mother-in-law and I, who usually get along fine, are chatting about camp. My son, who was probably around nine at the time, was sitting in the middle seat between me and his grandma when he dropped an absolute bomb.

He announces that today at camp there was this weird thing in his bag that was making noise, and when he pulled it out, he saw that it said Adam and Eve on it. His counselor snatched it away from him quickly. All I could do was just sit there, hands gripping the steering wheel and lie, saying that I had no idea what that item could be. My mother-in-law and I both just stared straight ahead. I couldn't look at her. I wanted to die of embarrassment! Not only was I horrified that probably most everyone in the car over the age of nine knew exactly what my son was talking about, but I'd also lost my vibrator, and now my mother-in-law most likely thought I was some kind of sexual deviant! I couldn't tell her that it was her son who had packed it, and used it, and then forgotten to unpack it, so I just drove. That had to be one of the longest car rides of my life. I just kept thinking, thank the Lord it wasn't a dildo! When I got home and told my husband what happened, he literally fell on the floor laughing. Needless to say, all three kids got their own duffle bags for Christmas that year!

I like the way it feels when hair gets stuck in my butthole crack in the shower and I pull it out. It tickles 👧.

A PRIME MISTAKE

Not long ago, I ordered my mother-in-law, who is not tech-savvy, a few things on my Amazon Prime account. I paid for them with her credit card and had them sent to her house. Have you ever been screwed over by your own online order history? Well, consider this a cautionary tale. A few months went by, and I used my Prime account again. I wish I'd ordered something nice and innocuous, like groceries or a few books. Alas, not that type of purchase. I ordered a vibrator. I was overdue for a new one, my husband was headed off on a business trip, and I was pregnant so I wanted (okay, I *needed*) to have a little something to tone down my hormones. I did my research and wound up getting something a bit, well, aggressive. What can I say? Pregnancy plus husband away had left me just crazy for any release. That's where things started to get a little bit awkward. Apparently, the card I thought I used for that purchase had expired, so Amazon defaulted to the last card that had been used on the account. As in, my mother-in-law's. Of course, unlucky for me that she is exactly that kind of woman who combs over every single charge on her statement every month and follows up on any random one she sees. She tells me about it and I confess nothing. I tell her it's no big deal, but she wouldn't let it go. She called the credit card company no fewer than five times and spent a whole day on the phone trying to dispute the fraudulent charge. I didn't know what to do. I couldn't confess it was me, and I certainly didn't want to confess to what I had purchased, so I went along with the whole fraudulent charge thing. I actually helped her fight this through the credit card company. Of course, she eventually got to the bottom of it, and her credit card company told her exactly what it was that was purchased on her card. Thankfully, they didn't reveal where it had been sent, so she never found out it was me. Of course, while she still doesn't know, she has been telling everyone that will listen that her credit card was hacked, whoever did it bought a sex toy, and this is why she doesn't like the internet. Every time I hear her tell someone, I sit there and cry on the inside, holding her grandson, knowing I will probably hear her complain about this for years to come.

JAIL MAIL

Everyone has a secret, but no one has more fucked-up secrets than a serial killer. I work as an investigative journalist and documentary producer, and a big part of my job is trying to convince people who have no interest in speaking to *anyone* about their heinous crimes to throw their caution to the wind and speak to *me*. Me, a bubbly blonde millennial in a mini skirt. This is not a particularly easy thing to do, so I've had to get creative on a number of different occasions to gain people's trust.

Recently, I worked on a project where I desperately needed to try to get serial killer Joel Rifkin to talk to me. If you're unfamiliar, he killed upward of seventeen women on Long Island between 1989 and 1993. He's a sick, twisted, terrifying dude. Guys who are locked up in prison for life don't have phones, so snail mail is the only option of getting in contact. Joel Rifkin is a relatively well-known serial killer, so I assume that he receives a lot of weird mail, including a few marriage proposals from those weird chicks who love murderers. I'm not one of those girls. This is business. And I don't fuck around with business. I *needed* this dude to talk to me, so my correspondence had to stand out amongst the bullshit.

I decided to print some new bright pink business cards that I could attach to my letter to give it some pizazz. But there was a questionable catch. Along with the personal info on the cards, I included a picture of myself. A picture in a sort of see-through shirt. With a push-up bra. And a flirty little grin on my face. And honestly, I looked hot as fuck. Sick, twisted dudes in prison love sexy ladies, right? As a little extra treat, I threw in some rose petals spritzed with my expensive Byredo perfume to really appeal to all the senses. As I sealed the envelope and sent it off to prison, I chuckled out loud thinking about my brilliant plan. I imagined Joel Rifkin's face as he opened my thirst-trap correspondence. There was no way he wasn't going to write back to his seductive new pen pal!

Was this at all dignified? No. Did I feel good about it? Definitely not. But the burning question is . . . *did it work?* Also . . . no. That piece of shit never wrote me back. I sent him numerous more letters and several business cards (you know, just in case the first one got lost in the mail), and . . . radio silence. But do you know who *did* write me back? Three brand-new pen pals locked up for life for first-degree murder. The first murderer said he traded an expired Twinkie for my business card, keeps it under my pillow, and kisses me goodnight every night. The second murderer legitimately thinks my original letter was addressed to him and is convinced that we're in a relationship. The third murderer just wrote "thinking of you" in what could only be described as the devil's handwriting and the letter was kind of . . . sticky . . . when I opened it.

So now I have to sit with the horrifying realization that my sexy business cards are being passed around the Clinton Correctional Facility as spank bank currency in exchange for a Snickers bar.

The moral of the story here is that the only thing worse than being wanted by a serial killer is being rejected by one.

I'M SO WET RIGHT NOW

This isn't *my* secret to share, but it's so fucked up and embarrassing I knew I needed to share. I was living in the DC area a few years back. I don't have a ton of one-night stands, but I've been known to have a wild night when the moment strikes. I met this guy out at the bar, and he was like six-foot-five, huge, athletic, cute. I was with another friend, who'd found her own conquest that evening, and we both decided to make a night of it. I was super attracted to my guy and really excited about the whole thing. We go back to my house and hook up. It was fine, you know, standard one-night-stand level of quality, but I was into him, so I figured I'd give him a second shot. I don't typically like guys staying over because I don't sleep very well, and I just don't like waking up with them at my place, but we managed to fall asleep. At around 5:00 a.m. or so, I hear him rustling around like he's getting up to go. I thought I heard him put his clothes on and then the door shut, but when I woke up two hours later, he was still there, lying in bed.

I figured, that's a little weird, but maybe he just had to go to the bathroom. Nine o'clock rolls around and this man has not moved. I finally woke him up and sort of tried to hint to him that he needed to go. I was going out with some friends later that day, and I wanted a few hours of uninterrupted sleep, but he just did not get the hint. He stayed where he was, in my bed, like a log. I started to get ready. Literally put my full face of makeup on, chatting with him a little as I moved around my room. He just sat there, not moving, from his spot. I'd had enough. I told him I needed to leave, so we could walk out together, and had to physically walk with him to the door. This man did not want to leave my apartment. It was so bizarre.

When I got back upstairs to take a nap, I realized why. My bed was wet. Not just "spilled a glass of water" type wet, but absolutely soaking. He'd clearly peed in my bed and then, rather than tell me, attempted to hide it by refusing to move. Or maybe he figured that, somehow, I wouldn't notice before he left, and it would dry before I got back. I ended up stripping the bed just mortified that this guy I'd brought home had peed in my bed, and then not had the decency to at least tell me about it. A few weeks later he hit me up, and we talked a little bit. When he asked if I wanted to go out again, I said something to the effect of "Hey, like just wondering why you peed in my bed and didn't tell me about it? Not sure I really want to do that again." Such a cringy experience, especially since he'd tried so hard to cover it up. I think if he'd apologized or offered to buy me new sheets or something I might have given him a second look. Big shocker: He never responded.

When I eat Cheez-Its
my vag smells like Cheez-Its.

PART THREE

LIFE IS TOUGH, BUT SO ARE YOU

Vulnerable Confessions
That Are Difficult to Share

This is the real shit. The secrets we have that we're almost too afraid to admit to ourselves, let alone anyone else. We push these thoughts down and down and down until they're a part of the very foundation of our souls. So much so that we sometimes let ourselves believe they make us damaged, or undeserving, or less than whole. Because these are the secrets that we rarely share with one another. We hope this glimpse behind the curtain can normalize some seemingly rare experiences that might happen a little more often than you think. We've checked our judgment at the door, and we're not gonna sugarcoat it or put some sassy catch phrases on it to soften the blow. To every lady who sent in a vulnerable secret, we commend you on your courage.

The very basics of keeping our head above water in life is not an easy fight, and sometimes just being alive is fucking hard. Figuring out where you belong in the world with work and friends and family and identity can be overwhelming. Getting old is a trip. The allegedly "beautiful" circle of life that makes being a woman so special through pregnancy and motherhood can be a brutal journey. So, if you've ever broken down realizing your body isn't working the way it used to, or you feel like you want to scratch your brain right out of your head, or if you've ever wanted to cuddle up in your most comfy jammies, suck your thumb, and hibernate forever, you are not alone. Our meat suits are slowly decaying every day, and we're just trying our best to hold on for dear life.

You could take all the antidepressants and go on all the wellness trips and master every yoga pose and still feel fucking broken inside. And that's okay. In gathering these secrets, we learned that depression and anxiety are the straight-up norm, and none of us like ourselves 100% of the time. Even the happiest person in the world has bouts of the "smads" (it's a combination of sad and mad, you know *exactly* what we're talking about) every now and then.

We wish all the secrets in this book could be funny stories about shitting our pants, but the brutal truth is that the world can be heartbreakingly awful to women. Even when women *do* muster up the courage to share their deepest and darkest moments, they are often victim-blamed, invalidated, or not believed. As women, we have become so comfortable with grinning and bearing very painful parts of life. We learn at a very young age to just stuff it down, pretend it doesn't exist, and move on with our lives. And as awesome as it would be to throw our painful and traumatic memories into a trashcan and ship it off to the dump, that's just not how life works.

Most of these stories fall into one of two categories: things we've done that we're not proud of, or the incredibly tough things we have gotten through that we *should* be proud of. Our hearts shattered reading you relive some of the worst moments of your lives, and we wish we could reach out and give each and every one of you a huge hug.

Lastly, we want to acknowledge that this next section of the book contains some pretty tough stories. If you are feeling particularly fragile or have recently experienced a trauma of your own, skip this section for now and come back on a day when you are feeling stronger.

JAC: SELF-LOVE IS A SCAM

I don't love my body. I know, I know, that's a super controversial opinion that really goes against this whole "self-love" movement going on right now. But I don't. And I'm sure you, my lovely reader, don't love your body all the time either. And it's okay to admit that. Because loving yourself is *not fucking easy*. Since childhood, we've been bombarded with messages that trick us into creating toxic relationships with our bodies. We grew up in a society that taught us to obsess over our *imperfections* and constantly compare ourselves to others, which created a perfect breeding ground for low self-esteem, eating disorders, and body dysmorphia. We grew up in a society that literally *profits* off of our insecurities and self-hatred. Add in social media, Photoshop, and face-perfecting filters, and you're basically taking one step forward and two steps back until the day you die. So, if you don't unconditionally love your body every single second of every single day . . . congrats! You're normal. You're just another victim of brainwashing by the beauty industry. And to be honest, it will probably take a lifetime to unlearn that trauma that society has inflicted on our self-worth.

Let's use cellulite as an example. For over three decades, during the most impressionable and formative years of my life, every single magazine and commercial and advertisement and woman in the world has told me that cellulite is *bad.* Do you really think that seeing a few body-positive posts in my mid-thirties is going to rewire my brain and erase all of the nasty connotations I have regarding those innocent little dimples on my butt? Even though my brain knows that cellulite is completely normal (as in, over 95% of women have it), to this day I still have a negative visceral reaction when I see my imperfect legs in the mirror. Multiply that disdain by every other *flaw* I have (real or imaginary . . . thanks body dysmorphia), and I'm constantly stuck in this hopeless loop of self-loathing and feeling lesser than.

Sometimes it feels like "self-love" is another oversimplified and overused buzzword that has lost a lot of its meaning along the way. At its very core, I get it. At the end of the day, when everything else fades away, all we have is ourselves, and we need to like the company we keep in the empty moments. And listen, I actually *do* really like myself. I think I'm a decent person, I am good to the people I love, and I treat everyone with respect. But that doesn't change the fact that I have been manipulated by the powers that be to have a super fucked-up relationship with my own meat suit. So seeing #selflove carelessly thrown around all over the place kind of feels like slapping a tiny Hello Kitty Band-Aid on a massive, gaping, blood-squirting-everywhere wound. Sure it's cute and colorful and sparkly, but it's just a distraction from the pain and confusion hidden underneath. And seeing other women embracing and loving their bodies on social media sometimes makes me feel guilty and fucking stupid for struggling to love my own. And then I start beating myself up for beating myself up. Why does it seem so easy for everyone else and so embarrassingly difficult for me? The shame spiral continues. Rinse and repeat.

What I constantly need to remind myself is that humans in general are dynamic and flawed and messy and complex. No one, and I mean *no one*, is happy with themselves all of the time. And though the intention is good, all the "love yourself, it's easy!" posts are still only projecting a highlight reel to the public. Because even the most self-accepting, good-vibes-only, glass-half-full badass bitch will occasionally feel awful looking at herself in the mirror or in a photo. And that's *okay*. And it's also okay to realize that trying to use a little bit of *positive thinking* isn't going to outweigh the damage that has been compounded onto our self-esteem our entire lives.

So, what's the solution here? Instead of practicing "self-love," I have started trying to practice self-acceptance and self-respect. And I'm not going to lie to you and tell you that it's easy, or that I instantly feel cured, or feed you any bullshit like that. But I'm committed to doing it regardless. I've started trying to focus on all of the rad things my body does besides how it looks. My body wasn't created to look perfect in a thong bikini at every angle. My body's *only* job is to protect my organs and *literally* keep me from dying. My legs let me take walks on the beach during sunset. My lips let me kiss my fiancé on the cheek when he brings me coffee in bed. My arms let me give my mom the biggest hug every time I see her. My heart lets me love, and love hard. My nose lets me stop and smell the roses. My body lets me do some pretty epic things in my fleeting time on earth, and it's time that I try to stop wasting time focusing on shit that does not matter.

Some days I wake up and I love my body. And some days I wake up and don't. But every day I will wake up and accept and respect my body, no matter what. Our bodies deserve to be employee of the month, every month. They deserve compassion, patience, and kindness. They deserve the extra five-minute foot massage. They deserve The Most Improved, Team Player, *and* MVP trophies. They deserve flowers on a Tuesday. Our bodies deserve a goddamn standing ovation. Every. Single. Day.

BECCA: BABY BLUES

I've been very open about my years of baby-making struggles, but there is one detail of the story that I have kept to myself. It feels incredibly scary to share, but I hope that by being open about it, anyone out there dealing with a similar struggle will feel less isolated. And maybe some of the guilt that I have carried around for so long will be alleviated, too.

After our heartbreaking first experience with pregnancy and the subsequent loss, Zach and I took a whole year off from trying to conceive. It took some time, but eventually we were ready to give it another go. We were lucky to get pregnant quickly, and we felt hopeful that we could finally put the last experience behind us and feel some joy again.

This second time around, I was about as early as can be when I took the test and saw the word "pregnant." I remember being at my sister's house, reading the test stick, and thinking, *This should be so exciting, why am I filled with dread?* I didn't have to be a psychologist to understand why it wasn't all rainbows and butterflies—trauma is a nasty bitch and she was lingering from our first pregnancy. What else could I do in that situation but accept what was happening, move forward with as much optimism as I could muster, and try to celebrate this widely accepted "miracle"? (Honestly, I'm not quite sold on that whole last part. A miracle for sure, but there's a lot of other really uncomfy shit sprinkled in there as well that no one ever mentions.)

Speaking of uncomfortable, I spent the next couple weeks barfing, barfing, and *barfing*. The nausea was so much worse than the first pregnancy. My most theatrical episode happened when I *mistakenly thought* that I had finally nailed down the one food in our house that didn't sound vom-worthy: water-melon. (That discovery didn't come often in those first couple weeks, so I was stoked!) I remember Zach and I were standing in our kitchen, casually chatting. I took a big bite of my "safe food," chewed it up into liquid-y goodness, and confidently swallowed it. When I opened my mouth to continue our convo—as ya do—no words came out. Instead, my voice was replaced by a violent waterfall of disgusting pink globs, shooting directly out of my mouth and onto our newly finished hardwood floors. It felt like I had actual demons living in my stomach, chucking the food out of my throat like a grenade launcher, and I was so over it. I calmly looked down, took a beat, and just walked away.

I can't know for sure if the inability to eat had anything to do with it, but with each day of my pregnancy it became harder and harder to get out of bed, harder to talk to people, harder to simply . . . exist. I had lost weight and the color of my skin was gray. I couldn't help but think, *Where the fuck is my glow?!* Every morning, I would wake up with what felt like a dark filter covering the lens of my eyeballs. I tried desperately to get up, move, call a friend, eat a cracker, anything . . . but I couldn't. My brain was my worst enemy, and I was starting to get very scared. Life just didn't make sense; it was dark and scary and I wanted out. I wasn't suicidal or thinking of ways to end my life—buuuuuuuut did the thought of a fatal car accident sound all that unappealing? Honestly, no. It was also a familiar feeling, nearly indistinguishable from how I had felt years ago while grieving a loved one who had died. Worse yet, that parallel left me super confused. Here I was, experiencing the exact opposite of grief—growing a *new* life inside of me, not mourning the end—so why was this happening? Logically, I knew that I genuinely wanted a baby—I was desperate for one—and that's what my body was giving me. So why on earth was I so despondent?

I started to do some research and came across the term "perinatal depression." Perinatal depression is a mood disorder similar to postpartum, only it happens *during* the pregnancy. I was fairly certain that it was what I was experiencing . . . the signs and symptoms all lined up. So when my sister helped me find a psychiatrist in Los Angeles, I felt the first relief I had in a while. This particular doctor dealt exclusively with women and specialized in treating pregnant women or mothers. Simply hearing that this type of person existed was such a comfort.

At my first appointment with the doctor (I was about eight weeks pregnant at this point) we were able to pinpoint that I was experiencing a "depressive episode," and she made me feel much better knowing that this was not as uncommon as I had thought. Honestly, how could I have even known it was common?! Who's on Instagram announcing that they are pregnant—oh and that also, like, life is meaningless and they're kind of apathetic about continuing to live in it? No one.

The doctor explained to me that anything was better for the baby than my current state. She also told me about an antidepressant that some women take during their pregnancies, and that it was safe for me to take it. It was really comforting to hear that was an option. I had never been medicated, so I told her I wanted some time to think about it. I took the next couple days to talk to Zach, friends, Google, etc., and I eventually landed on the decision to move forward with the medication; I would get the prescription at my next session. I knew it was the right thing to do, but I was riddled with guilt for needing this assistance. I just wanted to be "normal," and I was sad that the baby couldn't have a happier, healthier vessel.

The next week I had an ultrasound scheduled, so Zach and I made our way to our ob-gyn in Beverly Hills and sat down with our doctor to catch up beforehand. I explained to her what had been going on, that I had sought out the help of a psychiatrist, and that I decided to start taking antidepressants. It felt good when she supported my decision and agreed that it was probably the best thing for me, the baby, and my marriage.

With that squared away, it was time for the ultrasound. I laid down in my gown, Zach by my side, and she began the procedure. The doctor moved the wand around for about fifteen seconds in complete silence. This wasn't our first ultrasound, so we knew that wasn't a good sign.

After what felt like an eternity, our doctor looked up at both of us and said, "I'm so sorry. There's no heartbeat."

I started sobbing. Zach held me and we cried together.

Now, here's my secret. I cried because *I knew it meant I would have to go through all this again.* Those few weeks of pregnancy I experienced felt like I was serving a sentence: They were torturous. And now, that clock would have to start over, I was back to square one. Immediately after that feeling, a worse one came: relief. I felt free. I felt like I was going to get my life back.

I don't think anyone who hasn't experienced depression like this will ever truly understand, which is why I was very scared to share my story. People may think I'm a horrible, selfish, even crazy person, but I don't care. This isn't for them. This is for any ladies out there who might identify with these feelings. If no one talks about experiences like this, we'll never see how common they truly are. This is me telling you that it's okay, that we're okay. We are not bad or evil. We're strong and we're "normal," too. And my hope is that if more women start to share similar secrets, we may finally normalize these (very valid) feelings and help other women out there who are suffering in silence and shame.

KELTIE: MY HOLLYWOOD HEARTBREAK

I've had my heart broken enough times to understand the stages of grief that come along with loving something that doesn't love you back. But nothing could prepare me for the greatest heartbreak of my life: when I lost my job after a decade of loving it with everything I am.

To be clear, I am in *love* with my husband, and I *love* to eat Klondike bars and watch *Housewives*. The love I felt for my job was different. This job was everything to me. I put my work above everything else in my life. I skipped Christmas with my family so I could be the good worker and cover the holiday shifts. I didn't attend important weddings because I was "at work." I barely saw my niece and nephew for the first five years of their lives because I spent every weekend "on assignment." I rarely slept more than four hours a night and would often sleep on an airplane or in a car somewhere. I was obsessed with being the "yes" girl. I was obsessed with being everyone's favorite. I was obsessed with winning. As my work profile continued to expand, I moved further and further away from having any sort of balance in my life. I did not care, I had it all, even though most of the time I was stressed out, hungry, depressed, and crying in my car. I felt like I was the girl who everyone wanted to be, until I wasn't.

Show business and contracts and money and agents are messy and terrible, so I'm leaving out the details—but I found myself walking away from a high-profile job that had defined me for a decade and into the unknown. I was terrified. I was also filled with the most insane imposter syndrome. Out of nowhere, I was convinced I was worthless, had never had anything to offer, would never get another job, and had tricked everyone into hiring me for all those years. I felt like someone had died, but the person was me.

It was impossible to find comfort. Adele doesn't write songs about her boss. In fact, I felt at times, people were secretly happy that my magical bubble had burst. Life is mostly miserable for everyone, and my work trips to Venice and perfect hair and makeup on the daily were no longer triggering my followers on Instagram to feel jealous or insecure. It was my worst nightmare: I was normal.

So, I went to therapy. I saw a grief therapist every single Tuesday for a year. For one hour a week I was humiliatingly honest with a perfect stranger about how deeply, gut wrenchingly upset I was over a stupid job. For the first few weeks, I cried for the entire hour. I felt beyond pathetic! This therapist probably had clients who had *real* grief—people who had loved ones who passed away and other tragedies. And here I was literally spinning in circles saying things like "I thought they liked me!" and "but I always said yes!" "Will people like me if I don't have this job?"

The first step was to wrap my head around how much my life was about to change. I had done basically the same thing every day for ten years. The office had been my second home. The crew of our show had witnessed my engagement, my wedding, me buying my first house, breaking my first bone. I had celebrated birthdays, babies being born, and promotions, and had meltdowns with all of these people. I loved them. I was being ripped from my work family without a proper goodbye.

The second step, and perhaps the hardest, was figuring out who I was going to be now if I wasn't "three-time Emmy-winning host Keltie Knight." I was just Keltie. I had spent so much time being the best worker I could be that I had a "ships passing in the night marriage," "see ya when I see ya" friendships, no hobbies, no activities, no plans. I had no idea who I was without this job. I had been working toward the big time since I left my small Canadian home at age eighteen for New York City, and I had stomped on anything that had gotten in my way, including the things that would have made me a well-rounded person. I felt like the biggest loser on the planet.

But eventually, my therapist taught me to treat myself with compassion. I learned that I was not weak because I was sad. I wasn't a bad person because I had thrown all my human relationships to the side in order to be successful. I wasn't evil because I had wanted that success. I wasn't a monster who everyone hated. I wasn't useless now that I was no longer being used. I was not worthless because someone else didn't see my worth. I took my Emmys off my shelf and put them away in a cabinet. I changed my email signature. I threw out my business cards. I muted everyone I had worked with on Instagram so their posts couldn't trigger my emotions and make me feel left out. I shut off all my news alerts. I sold all my TV dresses on Poshmark. I let my gray roots grow in. When my anger would take over, I would run around my neighborhood until I had stomped out my mood. When my sadness took over, I would swallow a Xanax and go to bed at 7:00 p.m. When I felt motivated, I used the precious hours I once spent doing the job on reaching out to my lifelong friends. I created a little "goodbye big job" cocoon around myself. Eventually, like with all grief, I started waking up without the sense of dread that I had to try to exist through another day of pretending that everything was going according to plan, that I was incredibly happy, and that I wasn't a shell of a human.

The third step, and the most difficult, was the bravery and courage I had to pull out from the deepest parts of me to truly believe in myself. When the world treats you like a useless piece of shit, it's pretty hard to convince yourself that you are not exactly that. After a few months of wallowing and feeling sorry for myself in therapy, eventually we started to discuss what I really wanted in my life. I had spent my entire adult life waiting for someone to choose *me*, that I can honestly say that in all my years on earth I had never even stopped to really *choose* my own life. So, I dug in. The word that kept coming up for me was *freedom*. I wanted the freedom to love my husband, travel, spend meaningful time with friends, see my parents more than once a year for two days, the time to take care of my body and spirit, and mostly to get back out into the world and reinvent myself.

So, while I will forever be embarrassed that I sought out a

grief counselor for a job, I know I'm not alone in caring about my work. I did end up winning, by the way—just not the way I thought I wanted. And not to toot my own horn, but this new life I created is really, really good, and I can fully enjoy every moment of it because I am actually here inside the soul; experiencing life as Keltie and just being normal li'l Keltie is enough for me.

BECCA: A DAY TO REMEMBER

I moved to New York City in the summer of 2004 immediately after high school to attend The American Musical and Dramatic Academy, majoring in musical theater. I had received the most scholarship money available to an incoming freshman student, and my family was incredibly proud. As badly as I wanted to take the "road most traveled" by my sister and peers—attend an SEC school, join a sorority, tailgate on weekends, and basically have a blast for four years—I knew I needed to keep my eye on the prize (Broadway) and head straight to New York City.

For the first six months of living there, I was petrified. I kept a brave face for my family and friends because I didn't want to admit the fear, but I truly *hated* it. I didn't get on the subway once, I never left an eight-block radius between my dorm and the school, and I lost ten pounds because my dorm room was so disgusting that I lost my appetite just being in it.

I know I sound like a spoiled brat, but in my defense my dorm building was home to an interesting residential mix of students, elderly recovering alcoholics, and mentally ill, formerly homeless people who regularly brought literal garbage from the streets of New York onto the elevator and then into their rooms . . . with shared walls to my own. We also had communal bathrooms, and it wasn't uncommon to see an old man in his underwear heading into the commode to do unimaginable things. I could go on and on, but that's not what today's tale is about.

Even though I was miserable, I knew that this sacrifice was necessary for me to achieve my goals. I worked my ass off during those two years of the conservatory program and felt very proud of the work I put into honing my craft. And with time, I became more comfortable with the city, made some amazing friends, and even moved into "my own" 300-square-foot apartment . . . which I shared with two other girls.

After graduation, I immediately started auditioning for professional jobs and trying my best to get into Actors' Equity, the theater union for stage performers. I read the *Backstage* newspaper every day and wrote down the auditions in my little blue agenda every week. I took voice, dancing, and acting classes, and tried to see the occasional Broadway show if my budget permitted. I would show up for auditions at 6:00 a.m. and stand in line all day in the cold for the chance to audition for a union show . . . only to have the creative team decide they would not have enough time to see the nonunion performers that day.

After one of those very long days, I was finally seen for a production of *Cats* at a theater in Houston, Texas. The choreographer had us dance across the floor to check everyone's technique and then made the first cut. I made it! (Thank God for all those years of 8:00 a.m. ballet classes!) Those who moved on were to learn the full dance combination. The choreographer taught the combination at a rapid pace, no doubt testing our ability to pick up the moves quickly. I sweat my ass off in the jam-packed room of female dancers and nervously performed the combination when my group of four dancers was called.

After every small group had performed the full dance combination, there was another round of cuts, and then they read the names of the women who were invited to stay for the next part of the audition. To my delight, my name was called! I was to move on to the singing portion! I walked into the hallway and back into the waiting room feeling like I might explode from nervousness and adrenaline, and I warmed up for my song.

One by one, we went into the room, handed our sheet music to the accompanist, and then sang our best "sixteen bar cut" for the show's creative team (who were sitting behind a table, just staring at you). When it was finally my turn, I sang the song I had practiced with my voice teacher over and over and over again, and, thankfully, I nailed it. I had done everything in my power to impress the creative team and now the decision was in their hands.

I found out shortly after the audition that day that I got the job! All those hours of training, dollars spent in the studio and with my coaches were coming to fruition . . . I had booked my very first union job!

For the next couple of years, I did that song and dance (pun intended) almost every day . . . sometimes with the same magical outcome, but mostly not. I worked steadily in regional theater, and with every big Broadway audition that I occasionally would attend, I felt like the dream was getting closer and closer.

I was twenty-three when I auditioned for *Rock of Ages* on

Broadway. The audition was similar to the *Cats* one and to the hundreds of others I had done in those three years post graduation, but the stakes were higher. I didn't let that throw me, and I felt more ready than ever to finally be given this opportunity. Needless to say, I finished all the rounds of auditions, walked down the street back to my apartment, and within hours received the call from my agent that *I got the job!!* My Broadway debut was finally on the horizon. I sobbed uncontrollably with my best friend and roommate, Peggy, and called my parents . . . who also sobbed. In hindsight, I had no idea how much of a win this was for my parents as well. They had spent thousands of dollars and countless hours driving me around during my childhood preparing me for a life in this crazy and unpredictable profession. They were just as invested as I was, and now all of our hard work had paid off.

I remember this was the first time in my career that I felt truly proud of myself, like my talent and hard work had finally been validated. Before then, I had major imposter syndrome and wondered if I was just crazy or delusional to think I deserved a place on a Broadway stage or if I was even talented enough for one. (Don't worry, that syndrome returned many times after, but it was a nice reprieve.)

That night, I went out for dinner and drinks on Columbus Avenue with some of my closest friends to celebrate. Afterward, I was walking home with Peggy on cloud nine, and I remember saying to her that I felt a little "off." I had barely been able to drink my celebratory drink at dinner, and my breasts were so, so, so, *so* huge and tender. My period was normal-ish at the time but definitely not like clockwork, so at this point, I was around the time—give or take a day—that my period should be making an appearance. We were twenty-three but we weren't idiots . . . we knew we needed to stop by a drug store and pick up a pregnancy test just in case.

At the time I was casually dating a friend of a friend. I had known him for several years, and he was a truly great guy. I knew he wasn't my forever person, but he was funny and kind, and we had a lot of fun together. He was such a supportive person and knew how important it was for me to make it on Broadway.

Key plot point: A few years before this, my sister had been hospitalized and almost died from a pulmonary embolism. The doctors suggested it may have been a side effect from her birth control pill. My traumatized mom and sister demanded I come off of mine, too, out of precaution. So, the concern that I could be pregnant was real, especially when I remembered a recent encounter where the condom briefly fell off.

We got home and I immediately peed on the stick. It wasn't necessary for me to wait whatever the amount of time they say in the instructions because those lines came through long and strong right away. I was pregnant.

What were the fucking chances?? I found out I was pregnant the same day I booked my first Broadway show. (One of few jobs you can't actually do throughout a pregnancy, or for a long while afterward for that matter.) Not that I would have entertained the idea of having this baby if I had any other profession. I was simply not ready to be a mother. I still needed *my own* mom to help me "adult" at this phase in my life!

I had a friend who had just gone through all this, and she told me about an amazing center for women in the city where she went for her D&C procedure. I was so grateful to her and to that place. I wish more than anything I could remember what it was called, or even somehow track down the women who worked there, because they made a terrible day more tolerable. From my initial phone call, I was met with zero judgment, incredible compassion, and an overall gentleness. I strategically made my appointment for my first day off from the grueling rehearsals for my "new, exciting job." (How does that Alanis song go again? Something about being *ironic*?)

On the day of the procedure, my friend Peggy was by my side. To be fair, the guy I was dating graciously offered to take me, but I was more comfortable with my friend. He insisted on at least allowing him to pay for the $600 procedure, so I met him and his wad of cash on Ninth Avenue the day before. He supported my decision to have an abortion completely and agreed it was best for all parties involved. He was a very sweet guy. I was one of the lucky ones in this situation.

I don't remember many other details from the day . . . probably due to the amount of stress, fear, and overall shock I was feeling. I lay down on the exam table, and the physician gently began the aspiration process. It was only a couple of minutes, but the cramping in my abdomen was very intense. I squeezed Peggy's hand as I cried. I remember feeling so bad for the doctor who had to see girls like this every day. But, I also felt an overwhelming feeling of love and gratitude for this doctor who chose to spend her days supporting women through one of the most dreaded and difficult days of their lives.

Was it hard? Yes. Did my decision ever waver? Luckily for me, no. With that said, through the years, of course I've had those dark passing thoughts as Zach and I struggled to create a healthy baby. How could I not wonder if our infertility was some sort of karma for my abortion? I think it's only natural to feel that way, especially when in the depths of adversity. But do I *truly* think that's what it is? No. The reality is that it's just simple biology: I was twenty-three and super fertile, and now I'm in my thirties and, well, not.

I have a *ton* of resentment toward people who think that this decision can be made by anyone other than the woman who it is physically, emotionally, and spiritually affecting. I'm confident that if I had been a man at the pinnacle of his career—the very beginning of the *very* top of his field—society would never question or judge his decision to prioritize his career and his future over an unwanted pregnancy.

And for all the women out there who share this secret, I see you, and I'm sorry you had to endure that experience. I'm proud of you for being brave enough to make the unpopular decision for yourself. We don't often receive the message from society to do what's best for *us*. We are often made to believe that if we aren't the martyrs of society, we are somehow heartless or defective. Don't listen to that patriarchal bullshit. It was obviously created by weak, judgmental people. You are courageous, you are compassionate, and you are heroes.

KELTIE: FUCKING FORTIES

I do not want to be forty.

Whoever said that forty is the new thirty *lied*. All those female celebs claiming that "life really does start at forty!" are just saying that so they can appear to have youthful energy. Defying and/or rebuffing their middle age—ness is just a ploy to stay in the desirable column on the casting directors' lists—they all know that turning forty in Hollywood basically makes a woman radioactive and un-castable. Yes, I'm gonna genderize this, because—fun fact—this doesn't apply to men. They just get *more* great opportunities. Cool! When my husband got gray hair and gray eyebrows, he suddenly became even better looking. I started noticing hot, young women checking him out in public. No one says Brad Pitt looks good "for his age"; we just say Brad Pitt looks good. Ugh.

I have spent my entire existence in womanhood scanning the beauty magazine's "Your Best Fashion/Makeup/Skincare for Your Decade" articles. When I was in my twenties, I wore the advice like a badge of honor! I'm the freshest, the youngest, I can wear fun colors! The mags told me this was the age to take risks! And take risks I did. Overplucked eyebrows, box-dyed bleached hair, belts that I wore low on my hips and nowhere near my actual belt loops. My skincare routine was borderline crude: drink lots of water and use toothpaste as "skincare." What can I say, it worked! I would wake up every morning with a tight jawline and sculpted cheekbones no matter what had happened the night before. I was messy, dramatic, impulsive, needy, and it was *so. much. fun.*

I had huge plans and big dreams, and even though I was broke, trying hard was my currency. I could stay awake until the sun came up, sleeping for two hours, and then be a ball of energy the next day. I had sex in super weird places. I tried on a different personality daily. I had a general personality trait of being "excited about stuff." I was adventurous; I tried everything once. I owned almost nothing; I figured I had my whole life to get "stuff." I got myself into questionable situations and then added those near misses to my collection of "wild times." Mostly, in my twenties you couldn't tell me shit! I knew who I was, what I was doing, and I lived my life at a *ten* all the time. Even when I was messy, I was the most glorious, messy disaster the world had ever seen.

Then came my thirties, all full of possibilities. Sure, I wasn't the youngest, freshest chick on the block, but I was brilliant! Determined! Deserving! Had my shit together. But, when I scanned the same sort of decade-themed magazine articles in my thirties, life got more real. The articles sounded the warning that my past-due date was ever approaching. They made it crystal clear that we women must be doing *every available thing* to fool the world into saying, "OMG, I thought you were like, twenty-six!" Retinol became my best friend. And I spent thousands paying someone to point a powerful, painful laser at my face to burn off any proof that a life had been lived.

In my thirties, everything started deflating like a worn-out balloon. My lips. My under eyes. Even my butt turned against me and decided to make an entirely new continent called "lower butt." I now have a tiny mound of buttocks that lives directly underneath the firm lovely twenties butt that I took for granted in my youth.

To make matters worse, *Sex and the City* promised us (in Samantha Jones fashion) that our thirties would be our sexual revolution and that women don't even have the best sex of their lives until *at least* thirty. Again, total bullshit. My sex drive waited to catch up with me at the exact time I was layering forty-seven lotions, creams, balms, and hair masks before I took my four butts to bed to sleep on my anti-wrinkle pillow while lubed up like an anti-aging baby seal. I couldn't figure out why my husband didn't want to make out with me while I was wearing my retinol sleeping gloves, rubbing pain gel on my arthritic feet, and the ever-so-hot rocking my teeth whitening trays/reading glasses combo! What a mystery!

And now I am in my forties.

Forty feels like the actual end of an era. Everything in my beauty cabinet is "medical grade." Gravity has lengthened my entire face, my knees, and my vagina without asking my permission. (I want all the women with babies who feel like, "Those babies wrecked my vagina" to know that as a forties childless wonder, I can attest that no, your children didn't mess up your vag—the years did.) No longer do I get to *just* look good. I now "look good *for my age*." When I scan the magazines and see the "Fashion in your 40s" inspiration, it's full of grown-up clothing that is sophisticated, safe, and boring. I don't want to be a classy camel coat–wearing lady. I want to be young and effortlessly cute, I want to be fresh, I want to wear short shorts and ponytail bows. I want strangers standing in line at the airport to *wish* their seat was next to a "hottie" like me. I. Want. To. Be. FUCK-ABLE! What I don't want is to have to choose the skincare on the drugstore shelf that says "for mature skin" in big, bold letters.

Mentally, the tiny forty-year-old voice in my head is saying, *Well, I hope you did your best, because this is pretty much as good as it gets from here on out.* Sure, I'm inundated with inspirational quotes about such and such women who didn't even really "begin to soar" until they hit the big four-oh, but I'm enough of a realist to know that I'm just not remarkable enough to be ground-breaking at this age. I'm more of a "no fucks left to give" forties.

I'm tired and tired of trying. I'm tired of the rejection that comes along with big ideas and being a "go-getter."

Your forties are a never-ending cycle of waking up and feeling exhausted, drinking two cups of coffee, still feeling tired, talking about how tired we all are—then dragging our tired butts home and avoiding our workout because we are too tired. It's getting into bed early because we need to take care of ourselves, and then lying awake, filled with the anxiety of everything we didn't get done that day, a walking zombie of tiredness. On top of all this, there's also the guilt of not doing "the most" or enjoying every moment because life is *half* over, and the aging process is only going to slow us down even more. Forty is coming to terms with the fact that my best and brightest years are behind me, and the future looks like a leisurely stroll in learning to be okay with kinda being "eh."

I'm uncomfortable with the way my forties expect me to keep my emotions in check. I do not want to have been alive on the earth long enough to be the voice of reason or a mentor to anyone. People keep asking me for advice. They want to take me out to coffee and "pick my brain," and while I usually make up an excellent excuse and politely decline, what I want to scream is "IT DOESN'T MATTER WHAT YOU ACHIEVE! At some point you'll turn forty, and the world will toss you out with the elder trash so stop trying so hard."

So, yeah, I don't want to be forty.

Being a forty-year-old woman is awful, and anyone who tells you differently is lying.

THERAP-*ME*

Almost ten years ago, I was diagnosed with schizoaffective disorder. I struggled with mental health my whole adult life. It wasn't until I had a complete breakdown that I finally got a diagnosis. Sadly, after my breakdown and psychiatric hold, I lost several "close friends." I decided that I wouldn't tell people my formal diagnosis because I didn't want it to define me or for people to treat me differently. That time of my life taught me who my real friends were and to let go of what no longer served me. Therapy and medication have provided me with so much healing, and my life is better than I ever thought possible.

DADDY ISSUES

I actually wrote into the *LadyGang* podcast months ago that I was caught between my ex (who I had this amazing, unexplainable connection with, but we went our separate ways since he couldn't emotionally invest) and my current boyfriend (who absolutely adores me and wants to give me the world, though we have quite the age gap). The ladies told me to forget my ex and focus on my future. Well . . . I didn't do that. I cheated on my boyfriend with my ex, twice. Five weeks later I found out I was pregnant. My entire pregnancy, I had no idea whose baby I was carrying while pretending that everything was absolutely perfect between me and my boyfriend. When my son was born I was *sure* he was my boyfriend's, but now . . . months and months later, I still don't know. Some days I will think he looks just like my boyfriend, and other days I think he looks just like my ex. I don't know if I'll ever tell my boyfriend about this. Probably not—we are such a perfect family. And regardless—my boyfriend is my son's dad: He has raised him since the second I found out I was pregnant. But some days I wonder. I think it will be in the back of my head for years to come. Let's just hope we don't get some surprise from a 23andMe test someday. . . . Jesus, I can't believe I let this happen to me.

A YEAR AFTER I GOT MARRIED I REALIZED I HAD SETTLED. IT TOOK ME ANOTHER THREE YEARS TO MUSTER UP THE COURAGE TO LEAVE.

FRIENDLESS

I have no friends . . . literally not one. I make up things I'm doing with my "friends" when my family asks so they don't think I'm a loser. When my husband hangs with his boys I will leave the house to go out with "friends," and sometimes I just sit in my car in a parking lot somewhere till it's a good time to come home.

ONE IN FIVE ADULTS

I was seeing this guy (we'll call him Matt) who was so close to perfect it terrified me. We started to get serious, so naturally I got scared and bailed. I spent the next six months dating around while still crawling over to Matt's house weekly. I was on a certain swiping dating app when I saw an old friend of mine on there as well. His name was . . . let's say . . . Brent. We both swiped for each other and met up a few days later. We had a great hang out and an even better drunken first kiss. A few days later, we had our second date—which meant we got naked after a few shots. And after that I started to feel like something was wrong with my lady parts. There was pain, but also itching—and I noticed a sore. Deep down I knew what it was, so I was surprised how badly I sobbed in the doctor's office when they told me I had herpes. Matt was the first person I called. I told him I was sleeping with him and a guy named Brent, and I didn't know who gave this to me. Matt got tested right away and told me he understood and that nothing was my fault. He was negative. Brent on the other hand ghosted me and never spoke to me again after I told him, so that answers that.

I went into a pretty deep depression. Who would ever want to be with me now? I was disgusting and stupid, and I can't believe I put myself in that situation. I was once such a sexual person, and now it all feels shameful.

"

I wish my parents would die so I wouldn't have to feel guilty about not having a relationship with them.

"

THREE-YEAR NIGHTMARE

I was sold into sex trafficking by my fiancé.

He was charming at first—called me beautiful, pointed out how smart and funny I was, made me feel like a princess. He even proposed a month into our relationship, which at eighteen with no life experience had me over the moon and screaming yes. I was on cloud nine—but he slowly started isolating me from friends and family and accused me of being unfaithful if I wanted to spend time with anyone besides him.

I found out roughly two months into our relationship that I was pregnant. He quickly used this as a manipulation tactic to get me to do anything he wanted. Sexually, emotionally, and physically. Late into my pregnancy, I was balancing multiple jobs because I wasn't making him enough money.

Eight weeks after I gave birth, he told me we had no money, and I needed to sleep with someone so we could pay our rent. I refused, which made him angry and caused him to lash out saying I was a horrible mother because my beautiful two-month-old baby would end up homeless. The guilt became too much so I finally did what he asked. But in the middle of the first encounter, I asked the man to stop. He refused, so I just stayed where I was until it was over. Being raped by a stranger and then told how worthless I was because I was upset left me in the darkest place I'd ever been . . .

My partner told me he wouldn't make me do this again— until the next time we needed money. And the next, and the next . . . I'd wake up to random men in my bed—or I'd think we were going out to eat, but we'd show up to a hotel and he'd tell me the room number . . . it happened so many times over the years that I've lost count. Any time I would push back he'd threaten to call the police and tell them I was a prostitute and take my son. I lived this nightmare for three years until I finally left him in 2014, and I took my baby with me.

Three years after I escaped, I finally told a therapist, and she pushed me to report that I had been sold into trafficking by my partner. I had no idea that what I had been through was classified as anything other than an abusive relationship. The media and movies don't show the full truth of trafficking, nor the fact that over half of victims are sold by parents, a romantic partner, or a friend.

If you feel this applies to you or anyone you may know, *please* reach out for help.

USA—Department of Homeland Security at 1-866-347-2423
UK—the Modern Slavery Helpline on 08000 121 700 or the police
   on 101
Canada—Canadian Human Trafficking Hotline toll-free at
   1-833-900-1010

ADDICKTED

I have been sleeping with my boss for twenty years. It started when I was twenty-three and he was thirty. At the time, I was single, and he had a girlfriend. He later married her, and I got married as well. His wife passed away, and I am still married. No one knows. We have "ended" things several times—when he got married, I said it was over. I danced with him at his wedding. But we slept together the day he got back from his honeymoon. When things got serious with my now husband, it stopped for almost three years. And when his wife got sick it stopped—but it's almost like an addiction at this point, and I truly don't ever see it actually ending. This is the first time I have ever "admitted" that I'm a cheater.

I HATE BEING A MOM

My secret is that I hate being a mom. I never wanted kids but gave in to society's pressures after being told again and again how amazing being a parent is. They lied: They just wanted me to be as miserable as they were. I have only one child because it was awful. I wish other moms would have been more honest about how hard it is, and how your life does not belong to you anymore. I know I should be grateful that I was capable of having a child, but I'm secretly envious of those who can't. When someone asks me why I didn't have more kids, I lie and tell them I tried but it didn't happen. I HATE BEING A MOM. (I do love my kid, but it's been a struggle I could have lived without.)

POSTPARTUM DEPRESSION

Something I didn't realize would be so hard for me was having a baby. I've felt the need to keep my thoughts a secret because I oftentimes thought I was alone in my experiences. As long as I can remember, I had goals of having a career and having a full life aside from motherhood—but nothing ever felt so sure to me as the fact that I was called to be mom. So, I went to college, got a great job, married a loving man, all that good stuff. I just yearned to be a mom. I always imagined myself with like four kids. But now that I am a mom, I've had a bit of an identity crisis.

My baby's birth was sort of traumatic for me. When I went to my 37-week checkup, my doctor told me that, out of precaution, I was going to be induced that day. Sure, I knew my baby could come early, but three weeks? I probably could have refused, but I went along with it because I wanted to be safe. I was in tears, calling my husband to let him know how rapidly our day had changed. I had had a shitty breakfast that day, my hair was dirty, my dogs were home, I had nothing with me. I felt so rushed and unprepared. *I'm having a baby today?!*

My baby boy was born healthy, but much smaller than I anticipated. He had to be monitored for a few hours because he was early, but he ended up just perfect.

The first two weeks postpartum were my darkest days. I had intrusive thoughts, couldn't close my eyes, couldn't trust any of my family or husband to watch him while I tried to sleep for a few hours. It was a weird feeling—not really knowing what you are doing as a new mom, yet knowing that you know how to take care of your baby more than anyone else on earth. Sure, I enjoyed the cuddles and I loved my son, but the cloudiness from postpartum depression and anxiety made that time difficult to enjoy. I would sob in the shower, trying to grasp what the hell had just happened to me. As soon as the sun set, I would be filled with anxiety, knowing that a difficult night was ahead of me. Every two hours when he'd need to eat, I would cry because breastfeeding was so hard.

I started pretty much exclusively pumping, which, forgive the pun, fucking sucked. I just remember being so sad and feeling like a shell of a human, watching my family get to hold my precious son while I was sitting in a chair with a breast pump strapped to my chest.

I wanted to be able to nurse him like my friends could nurse their babies. The nurses were so strict about breastfeeding and made it seem like every drop was worth my sanity. They would tell me to nurse every two hours, then pump for fifteen minutes after each session. All right lady, when was I supposed to eat, sleep, or brush my fucking hair? I just remember feeling so low and crying while thinking, *What did I get myself into? What was I thinking? Why did I think I could handle this? This is awful. I thought I was meant to be a mother.*

Luckily, I have some amazing women in my life who texted me some beautiful and helpful words. Plus, I talked with my therapist, who prescribed some medication. I still feel like I can't tell people that I didn't always enjoy the newborn phase, and that the day he was born wasn't as incredible as I had hoped. But now that my little guy is five months old, I can honestly say it gets better. I'm so in love with him. I'm a little scared to have another baby, but maybe that will change.

Having kids is absolutely wild, and I wish I could give every new mom a hug. I can't say if other ladies will have a similar experience, or if the newborn period will come easily for them. But I *can* say that I am proud of myself for what I went through, and my life is so much better with my son in it. I look forward to the future. I know now that I was meant to be a mom—his mom.

"

I helped my
grandfather
commit suicide
when he was
dying from
cancer.

"

A MONSTER

My stepfather raped me every day from the time I was five until seventeen. He would leave money on my nightstand like I was his own personal prostitute. His fingertips are burned into my mind. I can still feel them sometimes. When I finally turned eighteen, I moved away, but he would send me text messages all the time saying that he loved me. I'm twenty-eight years old now. Sometimes I'm scared he stalks me. Sometimes I'm scared he will still hurt me. I've never told a single soul. As a young girl, I was scared to speak up. And now . . . who would believe me after all this time anyway? Who would believe the man across the dinner table at Christmas is a fucking monster?

PART FOUR

GRABBING LIFE BY THE OVARIES

Unapologetic Confessions That Deserve a Gold Medal

Ohhhhh baby, these are a *very* special kind of secret. These secrets are the kind we shouldn't really admit out loud, but want to scream about from the goddamn rooftops. These secrets are 100% led by that sneaky little devil on your shoulder. These secrets feel admirably selfish in a strangely endearing way; like if Reese Witherspoon was playing any of these characters in a movie, we would be cheering her on but not really understand why we love her so much. These are the types of stories men do *not* shut up about, but for some reason, we feel the need to keep them on the down low as women. When a dude sleeps around, commits revenge, get involved with a little fraud, or simply just *ages*, he's *strong and sexy,* but when a woman does the same things, she's crazy? Fuck that. From this moment on, we're not adhering to this ass-backward bullshit.

We can assume that every one of us probably has a gross or embarrassing story up her sleeve. But these secrets? These are the next level, gold medal secrets. We refuse to regret these stories, because honestly? We're not sorry. And that's what makes them great. The fearlessness, the brazenness, the I-don't-give-a-fuck-ness. If you dined and dashed out of your surgical bill, righteously hired a private investigator to take down a cheater, or catfished your own husband to force him to settle down with you, you *should* feel bad, but we also kind of wanna celebrate you? We feel weird and conflicted, but we're loving every second of it.

There is something very comforting about knowing that so many of you are a *little* bit shady. Because there isn't a lady alive who hasn't pushed her limits and broken the rules before. Whether you've gotten thrown in JCPenney jail for stealing a thong at fourteen years old, or you have to live with the fact that someone eventually bought that salt lamp that you licked at HomeGoods and it's sitting in their bedroom calming their anxiety at this very moment, it's good to test the limits of your moral compass every now and then to make sure you still have one.

Our motto over here at LadyGang is "you do you." Maybe you truly believe you're doing what is right (and maybe it is!). Maybe you have absolutely no other choice. Maybe there is a fire in your devious little soul that just *needs* to do "bad things" (hehehe). Whatever it is, YOU GO, LADY.

JAC: SCIENTOLOGY COWBOY

Looking back on my single days of using dating apps, I can confidently say that I met a total of *zero* decent men swiping through the fuckboy abyss. But if it's any consolation, I met a *lot* of hot guys who treated me like shit! Lucky me. And the best part was I let most of these sexy losers I barely knew hurt my heart and bruise my fragile little ego. This is the saga of one very special loser.

It all started while I was visiting my parents down in Orange County one fateful summer day in 2017. We were out for a cute little happy hour, so I decided to open Bumble to see the current pickings in the area. OC men were a *bit* more intriguing than LA men for a few reasons, but mostly because the majority of them had real, tangible jobs. I'm talking office jobs, jobs with health care, paid time off, 401(k)s, fancy titles, yearly raises! I even once matched with a man who wore a *suit* to work. *A suit!* Wow. Also, the male energy down there was generally more "laid-back surfer" vibes and less "Scott Disick is my idol" vibes. And swiping my way through the foreign landscape of Orange County to possibly find a soulmate was like an extra little treat while spending some quality time with my parents.

Even though OC was a fraction of a percentage better than LA, it was still full of mostly duds. But that wasn't going to stop me! Since it was almost impossible to meet anyone IRL these days, I was bound to meet my perfect man through the shallow, depressing medium of dating apps. So I started swiping. And swiping. And swiping. My thumb was starting to cramp up from all of the repetitive left swipes until—like an immortal god rising through the ashes of shirtless mirror selfies and drugged out tigers in Thailand—a chiseled beefcake floated to the top of my matches. Let's call him Taylor. Taylor was tall, dark, handsome, and had a *huge* neck, which is my ultimate weakness. Love me a blockhead! He had a super cute smile and worked for some medical sales tech company. He even had a pic of himself in a suit at some sort of work conference from a few months ago. A hot man. In a suit. Score! Taylor messaged me immediately, and we jumped right into some major flirting. He was smart, employed, handsome, *and* funny? Where were you hiding your flaws, Taylor? Underneath that thick head of hair? Or underneath your massive biceps? Or between your perfect set of teeth? Or underneath the big stack of money you make from your pharmaceutical salary? *Fuck.* As far as I could tell from my five minutes of interaction with him, Taylor was perfect, and I was not accepting anything otherwise.

Back in the day, when things were too good to be true, instead of looking at it as a major red flag, I instead thought it was the destiny of my much-needed fairytale happy ending love story extravaganza. It was finally *my time*; today was going to be the first day of the rest of Jac's and Taylor's lives!

I informed Taylor that I was in OC only for a short twenty-four hours to see my parents for the night. Because we were vibing *so* well, he insisted that we see each other *that night*. It would be a *tragedy* to wait for weeks and open up the possibility of letting our electric connection fizzle! Normally I would think this move was creepy, but because Taylor was so hot, I loved the assertiveness (yes, I know I'm a sucker). So I agreed to the last-minute date. He gave me two options and let me choose what I preferred: 1) casual drinks at a trendy restaurant in Newport Beach or 2) a fun night at the Orange County Fair. I obviously chose option two because . . . games! I am insanely competitive and insanely impressive at any and all games, so I was ready to show off my skills to my new potential mate. I *knew* he would immediately fall in love with me when he saw me effortlessly toss one of those germ-infested plastic rings right onto the neck of a Coke bottle. Ahhh, how romantic.

Taylor invited me to meet at his place before the fair, and knowing all too well the associated risks of meeting a stranger in a private location, I agreed immediately. He answered the door to his house (homeowner, check!), we caught eyes, and it was game over. Instant connection, instant attraction, instant *vibes*. We jumped into a hilarious discussion about whether the dress was black and gold or blue and white, had a pre-fair beer, and called an Uber. On the way to the fair, Taylor grabbed my hand out of nowhere, and I felt an electric jolt go through my entire body and into my lady parts. Our connection was so palpable that at one point our Uber driver turned around and said, "You guys are such a cute couple! How long have you been together?" Taylor answered "five years" and gave me a little wink and hand squeeze. I melted. He was a jokester *and* he felt it, too.

We spent the next few hours walking around the fair, grabbing drinks, eating fried foods, and having some incredible deep conversations about life and love and everything in between. He even invited his best friend and best friend's wife to the fair to meet me because he "thought I would fit right in with his group." It was quickly turning into one of the best and most validating first dates I had ever been on. He felt so comfortable, so reassuring, so empathetic, and . . . just . . . perfect. *Until he wasn't.*

After a few hours of gallivanting around the fair, Taylor

finally suggested we play our very first game. Geeeez, *finally*. It was one of those squirty water-gun horse-race games (not exactly one of my favorites since there isn't much skill I can show off, but whatever, this was my time to shine!). He paid for our round, we took our seats, and it was game on! With exquisite ease, the first drop in my stream of water hits right in the bullseye, and I was locked in. I held that plastic trigger down like my goddamn life depended on it. After twenty-six long, stressful seconds, the buzzer goes off and *I won!!!* Yassss, Taylor was gonna be so impressed with my skill, my focus, my determination . . . there was no way he was *not* gonna wanna throw me behind a poorly made roller coaster and fuck me right there in the dirt! I turned to Taylor with a smirk on my face and victory in my veins, pointed at him, and jokingly exclaimed, "LOSERRRRRRR!" And, as this was coming out of my mouth—in what feels like slow motion—I made eye contact with him and he. was. PISSED. He locked eyes with me, motioned his hand to the poor confused dude running the game, and goes, "Well . . . get your stupid prize." Wait, he had to be messing with me, right?? I chuckled nervously and said something like "Are you mad I beat your ass?!" and he just crossed his arms and refused to answer. Wow, okay, maybe we're improvising here? Some Groundlings shit. I *did* take acting classes when I was a child, after all. Ahhhh yes, obviously we must be role playing that we were in some toxic relationship and he was this fragile alpha bro. *Yes . . . and!*

The game operator exclaimed, "Since you had the fastest time out of *any* player today, you get to pick out one of our *giant* stuffed animals!" Yep, one of those four-foot-tall pieces of junk filled with Styrofoam. Hell yes! After some careful consideration, I decided on the giant banana wearing a cowboy hat because it made me nostalgic for *Bananas in Pyjamas*. I decided to name him Steve. He hands Steve over the barrier toward Taylor to help me grab it (because it was massive), and that's when things got *real* weird. After that tragic loss, a switch flipped and Taylor turned into a *completely* different person. This charming, silly, fun dude turned into an insecure, rude, butthurt douche bag. All because I beat him in a stupid game at a fair.

His fragile masculinity was light and bright for the rest of the night. He didn't say another word to me after that game. He proceeded to order drinks for *only* himself. We met back up with his friends, and he pretended like I wasn't even there. He straight-up *refused* to help me with my cowboy banana! And he walked five feet in front of me while I dragged poor Steve around at the fair. In trying to win some sort of redemption arc, he made me play ten more games with him, and I beat his ass in every single one. After every loss, he got more and more butthurt. Not my fault you suck, bro!

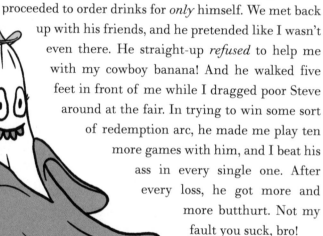

Because I was pretty drunk and really thriving in my victories, I didn't realize how insane Taylor's shift in personality was, and I never tried to escape the bizarre situation that night. But once it started getting late, I realized I was in a litttttttle bit of a pickle. My car was at Taylor's house, I had been drinking all night, and I was nowhere near my parents or my apartment to take an Uber to. And coincidentally, while we were walking toward the exit of the fair, Taylor grabbed my hand and turned to me and said in the sweetest tone, "You're more than welcome to stay at my place tonight." By the way, this was the very first time he acknowledged my existence in *three hours*, but because I was drunk and not thinking with any logical reasoning, and he looked super hot, I obliged. But you bet your ass I brought my giant cowboy banana home with us. I smushed Steve between us in the middle seat in the Uber ride home, and his little cowboy hat kept falling into Taylor's lap. Once we walked in the door, Taylor threw Steve on the floor (rude) and started making out with me immediately (not rude). What kind of fever-dream mindfuck am I living right now?! Because I had just gotten out of an unhealthy relationship recently, I jumped right back into this all-too-familiar "dramatically-fight-and-kiss-and-make-up" game. We made out some more, cuddled a bit, and fell asleep. Totally normal.

The next morning, Taylor kissed me goodbye and watched me struggle to get cowboy banana from his front door into the back seat of my car. He told me he'd text me after he got off work, and I went on my merry way. And then . . . silence. A week of crickets goes by from TayTay until my phone randomly lights up with his name. And this is the message that fucker sent me:

> Hey Jac! Sorry it has taken me a few days, but I just wanted to let you know that that was by far the best first date I've ever had in my life. I can't stop daydreaming about how awesome it was. I've honestly never clicked with anyone that fast before. You are intriguing, gorgeous and we had the most insane connection. So, I'd love to see you again. But, I'm not attracted to you, and I think we should just be friends.

EXCUSE ME??? WHAT THE FUCK????
I responded:

> I don't need new friends.

And that was it. I never heard from him again. After the complete mindfuck of my date with Taylor, I went on to date a handful of more losers, but his lame shenanigans always stayed at the forefront of my mind.

A few months later, I went to dinner with my friend Alexis at this restaurant in Hollywood called Franklin & Company, which was across from the Scientology Celebrity Centre. For those of you unfamiliar with Scientology and its presence in Hollywood, it is *everywhere*. And it is *invisible*. A good portion of the buildings in Hollywood are owned and operated by Scientology, but you'd never know it. They hide it under the guise of "personality centers" and "Psychiatry: An Industry of Death Museum." You can even go to L. Ron Hubbard–themed plays (I have and they're amazing; just make sure to smuggle in your own booze and never tell them your real name). The Celebrity Centre was the super flashy, super exclusive Scientology location that they'd flaunt their small handful of celebs at to try to appeal to unassuming innocent passersby. Tom Cruise, John Travolta, and Juliette Lewis would lead events at this location and really push the "Hollywood" of it all. That particular night, the Celebrity Centre was having a little event to lure in new victims by screening the new Pirates of the Caribbean movie. After a few gin and tonics, Alexis thought it would be a fun little activity to pop by and pretend like we were interested in joining the fucked-up cult of Scientology. A modern day IRL trolling, if you will.

We arrived at the front entrance of the Celebrity Centre, and that's when we realized we were trapped. A gaggle of Scientologists surrounded us and immediately demanded we give them all of our personal information. Our plan backfired. We were stuck. The walls were closing in on us, and there was no way out. I started getting tunnel vision, and that's when a lightbulb went off in my conniving little mind. When they asked my name, I calmly replied with a little wink, "Oh, it's Taylor! My parents love guys' names for girls" (which isn't a complete lie!). And since I was already down the rabbit hole, I tripled down. I gave them Taylor's email, phone number, and home address. I honestly probably would have given them his social security number if I knew it. I told them that I was *so enthusiastic* about joining Scientology and they could contact me any time! They could even stop by my house if they were down in Orange County because I *love* entertaining guests! And if you know the first thing about Scientology, you know those fuckers are *relentless*. They will harass you to join their cult until the day you die. And listen, I'm not a vengeful person. I'm honestly too apathetic to ever seek ill will against someone who wrongs me. But this opportunity for sweet, sweet revenge basically fell right into my lap, and I just couldn't say no! A victimless crime, if you will.

So, thank you, Taylor, for the worst first date of my life. I hope the Scientologists are still harassing you to this day.

BECCA: BUILT FORD TOUGH

Two weeks. It had been two whole weeks since Zach and I welcomed our baby boy, Ford, into the world via surrogate. Two weeks of vacillating between explosive joy and intense exhaustion. And two weeks of living what felt like every parenting cliché ever written . . . because, apparently, they are all true.

In the very beginning (i.e., the first week of Ford's life) we had my mom stay with us as an extra set of helping hands. Now, it needs to be said that she is an *actual* saint and quite possibly made of things ordinary humans are simply not, because whether the baby was cooing, farting, or screaming his face off until he was the color of a tomato, her only response would be pure love and endless patience. Honestly, if child rearing was all "nurture," I'm pretty sure I would have turned out to be the world's most magnificent person because I was raised by this incredible woman. (Lucky for you, my family history of mental illness—aka, straight-up insanity—made sure I didn't turn out to be nauseatingly perfect, but that's a different story for a different day.)

So after an amazing week with my mom, it took only four nights of just Zach and I caring for this new creature (or, as we lovingly refer to it, trying to keep a real-life Tamagotchi alive) for our house of cards to collapse. Here's a little rundown of how it went:

Solo night one: We fed him every two hours, as recommended by the pediatrician, and this angel baby slept peacefully between every feeding. I stared into his eyes during my designated feeding shifts and wondered what everyone was complaining so much about. Sure, I wasn't sleeping through the night anymore, but I had the *privilege* of waking up to this precious little face. I mean, weren't these the special quiet moments I would remember for the rest of my life?

Solo night two: Ford started to get a bit fussier between feedings and took longer to soothe, but in the grand scheme of things it was still a joy. Sitting in that dark nursery, I sang him the songs that my mom once sang to me. I took deep breaths and reminded myself how lucky we were. I was conscious to just drink in each moment and enjoy this time because we had waited five whole years for this gift, so there was no taking it for granted. (Not to mention, I didn't deliver this child and wasn't breastfeeding him, so who the hell was *I* to complain?!)

Solo night three: Okay, the wheels were maybe getting a little loose, but they weren't off the rails just yet. On this night, we maybe weren't our usual cheery selves as we passed each other between shifts. One of us didn't voluntarily stay awake anymore during the other parent's shift just to cuddle up and stare at the perfect alien in our arms. There were even a few moments where

I pseudo-snapped at Zach because I couldn't find a burp cloth or a pacifier during Ford's little upsets. We had yet to hit meltdown status (thank God), but Zach and I both could sense that things were hanging in the balance. We knew that in an instant, the magical mood in our home could take a hazardous dip. Well . . . iceberg fucking ahead.

Solo night four: Things. Were. Tense. Sleep deprivation was real AF, and it was taking its toll on us. In what felt like an instant, we had gone from a lifetime of sweet, uninterrupted, eight-hour-plus slumbers to *maybe* a total of three hours of choppy sleep a night. The thickness in the air was palpable when Zach asked how we wanted to handle the evening ahead. FUCK.

This was the point where we realized there was no "easier shift." His feedings were like sitting through a four-course meal at 11:00 p.m., 1:00 a.m., 3:00 a.m., and 5:00 a.m. every single night. Each of these feedings would consist of us taking him out of his bassinet after what felt like an eternity of squirming and whining, then heating up the bottle as he screamed and squealed every second that the nipple wasn't in his tiny mouth. Next, we would sit down and inevitably forget a burp cloth, but it was always too late to get up and find one because he was already chugging the bottle like a marathon runner on mile twenty-five. To make matters worse, Ford had started to spit up more after eating, so we had to feed him as upright as possible because of his reflux, which is really easy to do (JK) with a newborn who has no neck muscles and a core made of jelly. Essentially, I would spend the entire evening covered in dried spit and flop sweat.

After the feedings, if he seemed *just drowsy enough* to brave the bassinet alone, we would finally lay him down. This was when I was supposed to sleep, right? Sleep when baby sleeps?

WRONG. Instead of taking advantage of the quiet moments and sleeping myself, I was wide awake with thoughts like, *Are all these devices and gadgets we are using to monitor him—everything from the Owlet sleep sock to a sound machine—actually just creating a brain tumor in his little head from all the Bluetooth technology?* or *If this baby chokes on his vomit, will I remember the CPR I learned from the $300 course I took?* And as soon as I could calm my thoughts and start to nod off to sleep, the. pattern. would. start. again. Mr. Boss Baby was awake, and I'd better not fuck this up. This cycle went on and on and on . . .

It was during one of Zach's shifts when I realized we had become a newborn-parenting meme. I heard some banging around in the kitchen followed by many "fucks," exasperated breaths, and finally a grand slam of the door that goes out to the garage. I paused, took a beat, and for a moment thought to myself, *And this is what people mean when people say their dad left to pick up cigarettes and never came home.* Had Ford and I pushed Zach to his limit and he had finally broke???

It turns out, you can't run the bottle sterilizer, bottle warmer, baby formula dispenser machine (and all the other bullshit we had in our kitchen) at the same time because it would trip the circuit breaker. So Zach wasn't leaving us! He was simply going out to the garage to turn the power back on! Hallelujah! Honestly, it serves us right for being too lazy to do anything manually when it came to feeding and caring for our precious child.

So, yeah. It took me (only?) four days of parenting to realize I shouldn't have spent years internally rolling my eyes every time a mom friend warned me about how I wouldn't sleep again or how Zach and I would be at each other's throats over the tiniest things in the first couple of weeks . . . or months . . .

or years of parenting. I can't believe there was ever a time I assumed I'd be superior or more superhuman than all the other women of the world who raise children! But I consider myself a quick study. This arrogant and smug new mom may have learned her lesson the hard way, but thank god the learning curve was steep.

KELTIE: JULIA ROBERTS HATES ME

For an eighties baby like me, there is no bigger star than Julia Roberts. Best known as "America's Sweetheart," her wild hair, massive smile, and range as an actress have led to one of the most successful careers in Hollywood. She's basically the human form of a Krispy Kreme donut: *Everyone* likes her, and I grew up feeling like Julia Roberts was pretty much my best friend. Julia is so iconic that forty years after her movie role in the classic *Pretty Woman*, I still think about her every time I'm lying in a bathtub full of bubbles (don't act like you don't). How many times has someone reenacted the famous jewelry scene and snapped the jewelry case on someone's fingers just as they are about to reach inside? Or, on more than one occasion when someone has done me wrong, I have said out loud, "Big mistake. Huge!" just like her character does when she returns—post rich-girl makeover—to that snotty Rodeo Drive boutique. An Icon!

When this all went down, I had been working as a "journalist" on a nationally syndicated TV show and doing celebrity interviews for approximately seven years. To truly understand the story, I must explain the weekly workload of a correspondent on one of these shows, because while it was the biggest dream of my life, at the same time, it was all-consuming. I was flying around the world on red-eye flights, working at least six (often seven) days a week for ten to sixteen hours per day. Plus, I prided myself on being a hard worker and never saying no to anything. I once flew on a red-eye flight to the Bahamas, landed, dragged my suitcase across a sandy beach, changed in the bathroom, did my interview, changed back into my flying clothing, dragged my bag back across a sandy beach, and then flew home.

Working like this did give me clout. I earned a reputation as one of the "good ones" within the (often vilified) press. I was honest, I cared about my work, and I respected the publicist's demands when stars didn't want to talk about a particular subject. There is a fascinating and delicate dance that superstars do with the press in Hollywood. After all, we both need each other. It's a codependent relationship: The stars need us to keep them famous by talking about them, following their every move, and talking about what they're wearing or who they're dating, and we need the stars to stay exciting and allow us into their worlds to make engaging content for our shows. Overworking and holding myself to an exceptional standard translated to *access*.

Along came the most significant film festival globally, the Cannes Film Festival, and I was thrilled to be assigned to cover it. I mean, the *entire world* watches the red carpets of this A-list extravaganza every year. I was to interview Julia *and* her co-star in the movie, George Clooney. Now, it was rare to get one A-lister in a room for an interview, but to get two of the biggest stars on the planet together in one room, in France, well, it was almost unheard of! I had between four and eight unbridled minutes to sit with the stars in a little mutually beneficial kiki and pretend that we liked each other. The pressure was bananas. My never-ending impostor syndrome questioned my bosses for sending me to something so important, but at the same time I was incredibly thankful.

The first six minutes of the interview were wonderful; there's a reason that George Clooney and Julia Roberts are two of the brightest stars on the planet. I mean, they are extra-high-charm-level-super-wattage-sparkle-town. They have that special ability to make even losers like me feel seen, even though they are two of the biggest celebs in the world.

In that six minutes with George and Julia, I was pretty sure that we were on our way to becoming a new trio of besties.

At the time, interviewers were still allowed to "ask for a photo" after the interviews were over, which I planned on sending to the show's team to use to promote the interview. Somehow I ended up taking a "selfie" with George and Julia that broke the internet! The "selfie" had been invented by Britney Spears and Paris Hilton, but it was beyond rare to see A-list movie-star celebrities in "selfie mode." Most A-list stars didn't have social media accounts because being "basic" enough to have social media was for the less fancy "reality stars" and losers like me. Our selfie made headlines, and our BFF trio made the front-page news on CNN.

When my time with the runaway bride was over, I skipped out of Cannes singing "Oui! Oui! Oui!," knowing that I had been a major hit and had scored interview gold. This shine lasted about twenty-four hours before I was back in America and my "six days a week/sixteen-hour days and multiple movies/TV shows/books being read at the same time to prepare for the next interview" life.

My next "Bestie Julia" hang didn't happen until a few months later. Another Julia interview opportunity was coming up, and I overheard a producer say, "We should send Keltie to that. . . . Julia really likes her." Sweet magnolias, you should've seen me glow! I mean, I knew we had a special connection, but this was *My Best Friend's Wedding* level epic.

This press junket was for Julia's first-ever streaming series, *Homecoming*, on Amazon Prime. So of course, being the great, thoughtful, overachieving, A-type journalist that I am, I used the link the press team sent me to watch the entire series prior to my interview with her. A little note on how the "preview" world works. Often the press will get access to either the first episode or the whole series or be locked in a secret movie theater to view the movie months before the public. And, it is safe to say, only about 2% of the press actually take the time to read or watch the entire thing. Most high-level journalists have assistants who read/watch and then make notes on the important stuff to pass on to their bosses. I, however, am so K-type that I can honestly say—in the entire decade of my journalism career—I have read cover to cover and watched start to finish 96% of the projects I've ever interviewed a star about (even when I had to sit through all of *Transformers: The Last Knight*, which was approximately two hours and nineteen minutes too long). I did it for the greater good of the interview and the integrity I felt representing one of the biggest showbiz shows on TV.

Okay, back to my runaway bride.

Up to this point, Julia had set an absolutely unmatchable bar as far as her talent (*Erin Brockovich* for God's sake!!). So, when I finished watching that first season of *Homecoming*—and felt *nothing*—I knew that my bestie's long run of perfect hits had taken a questionable turn. By any other standard, the series was great. But, Julia is not just great . . . Julia is exceptional. Sorry not sorry, but I did not think the show was good. No one in the press would dare print a less than glowing review of anything Queen Julia does for fear of never getting another interview with her, so you will just have to trust a man named Jay S. on Rotten Tomatoes who said, "Very boring, Very slow, Could Barely get through the second episode," and another commenter Paul H. who said, "a two and a half star series at best."

All my preparation was for a three-day press junket event. Day one involved me driving to a hotel and setting up our two cameras for our one-on-one room. At events like this, there are multiple press outlets, and we all get our own rooms. The star then goes room to room, ten minutes at a time, and does almost the same interview with each outlet. It's very competitive for the members of the press because each outlet is trying to find a unique way to really make a "moment" with the star. It's also very challenging because there is truly nothing stars hate more than sitting in hotel rooms for fifteen-hour press days.

Press junkets are (at times) incredibly boring for the press, too, and there is a lot of waiting around for your turn. You set up your shot and then just wait, sometimes up to six hours, for the star to arrive. With all that waiting, there was so much excitement to finally be getting your "turn" that it was very common practice to turn cameras on as soon as you heard the star coming down the hallway. My team and I would always film the greeting; the little B-roll moment of the star walking in and shaking hands with me (the host) and the small-talk welcome. Most of the time, we never use that footage. It's pretty boring. But magically, on this day, just as we were rolling on Julia settling in to start the interview, none other than Dermot Mulroney walked by the hallway while our cameras were rolling and came into our room to greet her! Again, this seems so silly that this would even matter, but the press are oftentimes feasting on scraps trying to make things seem bigger or more exclusive than they are. I don't remember what they said to each other; it was very bland and basic. I think they mentioned seeing each other at lunch and that was that . . . but we did get it on tape.

My interview went well, and Julia was giggling and smiling her megawatt smile. I had come up with a neat idea for a story since this current project, *Homecoming*, was her third project with dreamboat bestie Dermot. With *My Best Friend's Wedding*, *August: Osage County*, and now *Homecoming*, their trifecta consisted of a romantic comedy, a drama, and now, finally, a thriller. The question was simple: "Do you think you'll ever complete the circle and do another rom-com?" to which she replied, "Well you know at a certain age it gets hard to believe that someone can be so naïve in love." It was a really smart non-answer and, technically, I couldn't agree more. When my forty-year-old friends have twenty-one-year-old level boy trouble, I just roll my eyes and think, *oh my God have you not grown up at all!* And, even though I'd still watch an octogenarian Julia Roberts fall in and out of love on the big screen, she made a good, albeit vague, point. The interview ended, and I packed up my stuff and headed home to start watching whatever movie/book/TV thing I had to watch to prepare for my next press junket (which happened to be the next day).

A couple days later was the big red-carpet premiere for *Homecoming*. So, I got all glammed up and arrived super early to our 12 x 12 platform outside the theater to wait for "The Queen." (See, there *is* a lot of waiting in this job.) She stepped out wearing an amazing hot pink pantsuit (put together—of course—by her longtime stylist Elizabeth Stewart). Combined with her trademark big hair, she dazzled on the carpet in the way that only Julia Roberts can. Next, it was time for her to do her two-minute interviews with each of the press outlets and, even though I had been standing there for hours waiting for her, *she walked directly past me . . .* not even looking in my direction! I was shocked. I assumed the skip was some sort of horrible mistake, so I sent our producer down to talk to her team. The news was horrible. "Julia's not doing you." I was flabbergasted. I begged for a reason. Their response? She wasn't happy with the way I used that footage of her and Dermot saying hello and thought it was very unprofessional. And she wasn't happy about my headline.

OMG.

At that moment, the interview flashed before my eyes, and I just couldn't understand how the hello with Dermot was a big deal. It showed that she was just a normal person and that her relationship with Dermot was real. It's not like we secretly filmed her having a meltdown and throwing a cell phone at someone's head, ya know? We literally showed her being the loveliest, kindest, friendliest friend on the planet. (And, sorry not sorry again, I still stand by my show using it.) It is important to note, too, that once I finish an interview, I very rarely have anything to do with the final cut of the story. The footage of my interview gets sent to the news team and the online team, and then an entire staff of producers and writers takes over. The divisive headline in question was "Julia Roberts Explains Why She Shouldn't Star in Rom-Coms Anymore." (Go ahead and google it; you know you want to!) I still feel like that's an appropriate headline to represent what she had said to me that day. However, what happened next—and probably what she was referring to—was totally out of my control. *Every single press outlet* in the world took my interview and repurposed it with their own more clickbait headline. *InStyle* magazine was first: "Julia Roberts Is Done with Rom-Coms." Next Yahoo! posted, "Julia Roberts on Why She's Done with Rom-Coms for Good." *Time* magazine's version was, "Julia Roberts Says She's Done with Rom-Coms for Good." And on and on. Like a tricky game of telephone, the international press took my interview and turned it into something that it wasn't and turned a headline into something that she simply did not say.

But I couldn't say any of this. Instead, I apologized profusely. I pleaded. I told her team that if I didn't get an interview with Julia Roberts tonight, I was probably gonna lose my job (which was the truth). Her team, though lovely, said they would ask her again, but it was not likely she would talk to me. I was dumbstruck.

Then, out of the corner of my eye, I saw hot pink fabulousness coming my way. Julia had changed her mind! The interview was on! What happened next was the worst two minutes of my career and something that I have watched on repeat multiple times in a dark office from the vault of footage that I hope never sees the light of day. *The* Julia Roberts stood with me and called me out on my alleged fraud—directly on camera with a microphone in her hand—on a live feed that went out to every CBS station in America. She said through her big, beautiful smile, "You put words in my mouth." And then she just stood there waiting for my response.

I've lain awake and spent therapy sessions reliving and redoing this interaction multiple times in my head. My best self would have said, "Julia, what are you talking about? These headlines are a game of telephone. Just look here, I googled it on my phone and *my* headline doesn't say that!" What I should've said was, "Julia Roberts, you've been famous long enough to know that a little loser interviewer has zero to almost no power as to what makes it on the air. Also, I *know* you are smart enough to know that any time you walk into a room anywhere when your hair is curled and your mega white smile is on display, you are probably being filmed." But, I was my *worst* self that night. Overworked, overtired, confused, and in the moment unsure if we *had* made up a headline, I just blabbered, "I'm so sorry, I am I'm so sorry, I mean . . . we . . . but . . . just, yeah. What a great night here it is! You look gorgeous!"

(For the record, I *can* absolutely understand how, after being in show business for decades like she has, this sort of thing must happen constantly. It's got to be super frustrating to read headlines about yourself and things you allegedly said, but never did. But—and I want to be perfectly clear—I never said that Julia Roberts was done with rom-coms.)

So the secret is this: Julia Roberts hates me.

Julia, if you're reading this (which I know you're not because I'm sure Oprah sends you a curated selection of books each month, and this book is *not* going to be one of them), I'm really sorry about this whole mess. I haven't been able to look at our "Cannes Film Festival bestie" selfie with the same adoration and giddiness since. *Homecoming* went on to be a mediocre snooze fest that no one talked about and you left after one season, so sorry not sorry my instinct was probably right. But, then again, you are rich AF, have an Oscar, and are actual BFFs with George Clooney, so I know you give zero fucks about my stupid opinion. The *extra bonus* secret of the story is that being a member of the press is *the worst*, and it's essentially like being an overdressed punching bag; the delicate dance the entertainment news press does is often an uncomfortable nightmare filled with anxiety, desperation, self-remorse, and the feeling that you did something wrong when you actually didn't. I know in my gut that I didn't do anything malicious or harmful to my queen Julia, but I also have to live with the fact that I've never been asked to interview her since. The worst part? I don't think we are getting a *Notting Hill 2*, and it's all my fault.

BECCA: THE MAID OF DISHONOR

My childhood best friend was getting married, and it was set to be a magical day from start to finish. Let me be clear, by "magical" I mean I was stoned by 11:00 a.m., met with my own *personal* chicken nugget tray the moment I entered the bridal suite, and was surrounded by some of my favorite humans on the planet. The bride was one of my oldest and dearest friends, and I was so happy to be witnessing (with glassy eyes) the happiest day of her life. TBH, she deserved all the happiness in the world after dating some huge losers (drug dealers, "musicians," etc.) in her twenties. This day needed to be perfect, and I was taking my bridesmaids duties very seriously.

The bride was a real sucker for rituals and traditions so, as we all were getting ready, she was checking off her list all the things she needed to be wearing, eating, carrying, saying, etc. for the big moment. At the top of the list was her late grandfather's "lucky penny." To be clear, this penny was never a possession of her grandfather's. She had found it in the days following his passing, and it was her belief that this was him saying hello from the other side—I guess pennies were their thing. Anyway, I couldn't care less how she wanted to honor her late grandfather—live your life, boo. I loved him, too.

And, while the sentiment was very sweet, it is also important to note that the lovely bride had a flair for the dramatic (bless her heart) and took the passing of her very old, lived-a-full-long-life-into-his-eighties grandfather *very* hard. The mere mention of his name during the wedding weekend was met with the same tone and emotion reserved for a teenager being taken too soon in a tragic car accident. (And yes, the lack of empathy on this topic is a major flaw of mine. I'm aware.)

So, it was moments before the walk down the aisle, and the bride (she isn't the greatest under pressure, either) was already breathing in an alarmingly shallow manner and speaking in a hurried, slightly manic tone. All the anticipation from the seven hours of getting ready mixed with the gallons of champagne wasn't boding well at the moment.

Finally, it was time for us to move toward the aisle. Hallelujah. But, just as my friend was heading for the door, I heard a shrill scream and something that resembled "Pop's penny!!" I looked over my shoulder and saw the bride reaching into her bodice, jamming her hands up her skirt into her underwear, and finally searching the floor around her. She had lost Grandpa's lucky penny!! FUCK!

I knew deep down that finding this penny would be like finding a needle in a haystack . . . but this stunning bride was unraveling. I could see the situation taking a very dark turn; we needed to get this show on the road and avoid a nuclear meltdown. So I did what any great bridesmaid would do: I reached into my wallet to find the oldest, rustiest, darkest-looking penny in there, then crouched to the ground and screamed "Found it!!!"

In retrospect, I'm fairly certain my best friend knew this was not *the* penny, but I think she was grateful that the issue was "solved" and was ready to marry the man of her dreams and black out on the dance floor . . . or at least that's what I tell myself.

JAC: JOSH SQUARED

I'm extremely uninterested and unphased when it comes to celebrities. This is news to absolutely no one. I could be sitting next to Harry Styles and wouldn't look twice at him. The only celebs I care about are the cast of *Lost*, Larry David, and Guy Fieri. No more, no less. So it is pretty ironic that I live smack dab in the middle of Los Angeles, the epicenter of the beautiful and famous. In fact, at this very moment, I'm writing this story at a café in Venice sitting ten feet away from where Jonah Hill is enjoying a cup of coffee. But that's just your typical Tuesday in

La La Land! Celebrities walk among the common folk, and we pretend to not notice them, all while trying to eavesdrop on their most private conversations.

And just because I don't care about celebrities doesn't mean I don't see them. I actually love a good celebrity encounter, but I rarely talk about them openly. And that's because there is this bizarre unspoken rule in Hollywood that you *never* publicly talk about experiences with celebrities, *especially* a romantic or sexual experience. God forbid you break their squeaky clean veneer! Privately to your besties, let it rip. But if you dare to spill the tea about a celebrity, you are opening your life up to a potential world of hell. I'm talking trolling, cease and desists, lawsuits, death threats, you name it. It's literally why anonymous submission celebrity gossip accounts like Deuxmoi exist. People ask the account to post their celeb sightings with the note "anon pls" because everyone is too scared to publicly share that they saw Paul Rudd ordering broccoli cheddar soup at Panera Bread. Everything is *allegedly,* or you use *pseudonyms* or *nicknames* when talking about celebrities to avoid getting sued for slander.

So with that being said, this is the story about how I accidentally went on a date with Josh Duhamel. Fuck it, right?! Please don't sue me, Josh.

It all started on one warm, sunny afternoon, when we (the LadyGang) were prepping a packed lineup for our podcast. For those of you that don't know, our podcast started as a "celebrity-driven show." So because I'm pretty useless on the topic of celebs, I always personally prep by doing a quick little google before every episode to get the very bare minimum basics in my brain so I don't embarrass myself and ask Blake Lively if she's single or not. That day, our recordings looked a little something like this: Carmen Electra, Michelle Williams, Gigi Gorgeous, and Oliver Hudson. Hold up, Oliver Hudson? A *man*?? We *rarely* had men on the show, and when we did, they usually were into other men sexually, so I needed to do a deep dive to figure out if I had to wash my hair that day or not.

Google: Oliver Hudson

Google: Oliver Hudson height

Google: Oliver Hudson married

Good news: Oliver Hudson is six-foot-one. *And* straight. *And hot.* Bad news: Oliver Hudson was married. And had been for fifteen years. FuUuUuUcK. However, I was still *very* excited about the idea of having any kind of interaction with a hot man because I was extremely desperate and attention deprived. So, I washed my hair, put on mascara *and* lip gloss, and even changed out of the trash bag I usually wear for our podcasts into a pair of leggings and a crop top. In my fury of trying to look presentable, I forgot to look up anything about Oliver's life. So, I was *really* going into this situation completely blind, but at least I didn't look like the creature from the black lagoon.

Oliver shows up to the studio, and he was just as hot as Getty Images made him out to be. Turns out Oliver Hudson is Kate Hudson's brother and a successful actor. Huh. Who knew?! And the real zinger was he was super charming and funny as hell. This all made me really pissed about the whole marriage thing but really happy I put on deodorant. We jumped into the podcast with all the usual questions about career and success and failure, etc. And then at some point, the conversation turned to me being soul crushingly single . . . and if Oliver had any friends to hook me up with. To my utter surprise, he immediately responded that he had the *perfect* dude for me: his good friend Josh. Josh was twelve years older than me, an entrepreneur, and was genuinely looking for love. He said that Josh's biggest downfall was that he was truly searching for a *real emotional connection* with a partner and wasn't into the surface level bullshit. I mean, could you *die?!* Every woman is looking for a Josh! Oliver's enthusiasm for Josh as my soulmate was through the roof despite knowing zero about me. But I was in. JAC & JOSH 4EVER.

We tried to move on, but the conversation just kept shifting back to Josh, as Keltie, Becca, and I needed to investigate my mysterious new love interest. And every single new fact I learned about him solidified that he, in fact, *was* my soulmate. A few examples:

I jokingly told Oliver that Larry David was my dream man.

Oliver's response: "Josh is such a huge LD fan that his email is literally LarryDavid@hedidnttellusthewebsite.com." This was a huge win because I literally watch *Curb Your Enthusiasm* every night to fall asleep. My future partner had to be cool with Larry David lullabies.

Keltie asked if Josh would be down for drinking at 10:00 a.m., my favorite time to enjoy some libations.

Oliver's response: "Not only does he love day drinking, but *he makes his own wine*." Double win! I was gonna have a new boyfriend, and I'd also save *thousands* of dollars a month on drinks!

Becca asked if Josh liked to travel.

Oliver's response: "He loves Europe [LOL who doesn't?], and he just opened up a new hotel off of the Santa Barbara coast." Another money saver! Who wanted my measly hotels.com points?!

Keltie asked where Josh lives.

Oliver's response: "In Venice." *Five minutes away from me.*

Now, this one was a huge deal because dating outside of your neighborhood in LA is honestly worse than dating outside of your country. At least the latter has the option of a dual passport and a sexy accent.

I asked if he was into true crime, because I am a true-crime *freak* (so much so that I started my own true-crime podcast).

His response: "Not only does he like true crime, but Josh used to be super good friends with Scott Peterson and would go golfing with him all the time." *What!* Who the hell was actually *friends* with Scott Peterson?! I needed to meet Josh just to interview him about *his* whereabouts on December 24, 2002.

This was all too good to be true. These #joshfacts were really throwing me for a loop. Oliver then showed us a few pics of Josh. One was literally the back of his head, and the other looked like a LinkedIn thumbnail from 2002. He said Josh had Instagram but never used it. Ooooooh, a man off the grid. I could get down with that. We ended the podcast joking that Oliver was gonna have to bring Josh on the podcast for our first date, and then we went our separate ways.

Oliver quickly connected me to the elusive Josh, and other than these random factoids, I knew absolutely *nothing* about him beforehand. He didn't give me Josh's Instagram or last name so I had zero ammo for stalking, which really stressed me out. I tried to google "Oliver Hudson Josh," but the only shit that came up was Oliver and Josh Duhamel (more on that later). But regardless, I was *living* for this whole situation. Nothing gets me riled up more than going to the absolute extreme in my mind and fantasizing what a *hilarious and quirky* story this would be at our wedding someday (maybe Kate would be my bridesmaid??). And if you're rolling your eyes thinking I'm a desperate loser, you're a liar because WE ALL DO THIS with every Bumble match we get.

So, Josh and I started texting. He was funny and charming, and had great banter. Check, check, and check please! We finally decided on a day for our date, and Josh suggested a Saturday brunch—ummm, excuse me? Are you my soulmate because I *fucking love brunch*—and it was in that moment that I truly realized my bar is on the actual ground and I really should think about raising my standards one day, but whatevs. Not today! Stoked on the brunch. And more important, I was excited to use my evil genius mind to craft the perfect outfit that would show the right amount of skin to be sexual but also would leave enough to the imagination (trust me, it's an art). I finally decided on a balloon sleeve, plunging V-neck crop top and a pair of those slinky bell bottom pants that make *any* butt look like a ripe-ass peach. (You know the pants . . . but if you don't, google "Novella Royale Janis Bells" and thank me later.)

Josh suggested we should ride our bikes to brunch, which was adorable, but I was also secretly worried about getting a BUI (you know, Biking Under the Influence, which, by the way, holds as much weight as a DUI). If you read our last book, you *know* I can't go on a date sober. Three brunchie-mimosa minimum, please! But, I gave in to biking as our form of transportation because my butt looked reeeeeeal good in those pants, and I couldn't miss out on an opportunity for my booty to be bouncing around if we hit a speed bump!

So Josh met me at my tiny, dilapidated apartment in Venice (which costs more than a mansion in Idaho), and we made our way out into the world. I'm going to fast forward through the brunch portion of the day because most of it has fizzled from my memory (there's only so much space in there, and I need room for *90 Day Fiancé* conspiracy theories). Basically, he was a total gentleman, we had good conversation, and he paid for brunch. Definitely not the "love at first sight/I want to jump your bones" connection I was hoping for, but oh well. Sometimes love has to blossom or whatever.

I will, however, *slam* the pause button on the moment Josh told me he was gonna text *his* other friend Josh to come meet us. It is not, under any circumstances, a good sign when the dude you're on a first date with wants to invite one of his friends to join. It usually means he's not into you but is too nice to break the news, and is ready to turn the opportunity of a romantic moment into a *bro hang*. Fantastic. Josh did preface the invite by telling me that his friend was having some girl troubles and needed a good dose of friendship, so the empath in me felt for the dude and accepted the third wheel. And to be honest, I wasn't that bummed because mine and Josh's connection was *meh* at best. Guess I was one of the bros now! *Pass the beer bong.*

But two Joshes?? That's a lot. And I was kind of drunk already. How would I tell them apart? I was gonna need a nickname in my head to decipher one from the other after all of these mimosas. Josh 2.0? Josh the Second? Sad Boy Josh?

Turns out, I wouldn't need any special mnemonic devices to tell them apart because Josh's friend was *Josh fucking Duhamel.* Yeah, you read that right. And if you're wondering, yes, *that is* a celebrity I recognize and care about. Mostly because he's six-foot-four and a total hottie, but also because I was *obsessed* with *Win a Date with Tad Hamilton!* for some unknown bizarre reason when I was younger.

So anyway, Josh Duhamel was now officially a third wheel on

my brunch date. He even brought his own bike, so he was committed to the hang. The three of us spent the rest of the afternoon gallivanting around Venice with the wind in our hair and my butt bouncing on my seat (God, I was *so* glad I wore those pants). Josh 2.0 vented to us about his girl problems; we gave him advice and bought him drinks like any good besties would do. My chilled-out energy and general apathy in life really worked in my favor that day because I was absolutely slaying it on this two-on-one (who do you think I will give my rose to at the end of the night?). I was cracking jokes, offering up an objective girl perspective, and being an overall general delight (I think? Again I was pretty drunk, so who knows). But of course, secretly in the back of my brain I was scheming how to really flip the script and convince Josh #2 that Jac Vanek was the *perfect* rebound for him. *Oh, how the turn tables.* I wonder what Oliver would think of this Josh switcheroo! I'm not even religious, but I went into the bathroom and did a little mini prayer thanking the big guy upstairs for the lackluster connection with Josh #1.

The whole day ended up being a total blast. We bar hopped around the West Side, we took silly photos for Instagram (and I commented on Josh Duhamel's saying "photo credit!" like the absolute embarrassment I am), and we even went to a super fancy dinner at this restaurant called The Tasting Kitchen. And during this meal I was literally sitting in the middle of both of the Joshes at the bar like I was the goddamn Bachelorette being like . . . how did I end up here? What the fuck is my life right now?! What was I supposed to do with this opportunity? Was this my fate? Were we going to have a threesome?? I took all of these existential questions into account and decided that maybe I *could* make out with Josh Duhamel that night. Josh #1 was 100% in the friend zone in my mind. It was *his* fault for inviting Josh 2.0 on the date, and I was ready to take full advantage of his mistakes. So I ordered an expensive glass of rosé and really tried to turn on the Jac charm.

Spoiler alert: I didn't make out with Josh Duhamel. He didn't even give me his phone number or follow me on Instagram. Looking back, the only thing he cared about was hanging out with Josh #1 that day. There is a *zero* percent chance he even remembers I was there or has any idea who I am. So, is it a mistake to permanently publish my accidental date with Josh Duhamel in this mediocre memoir? Maybe. Honestly, people have been sued for much less. But like I said before, *fuck it.*

The real moral of this story is *never* invite Josh Duhamel to be a third wheel on your date. *I'm talking to you, Josh #1.*

KELTIE: MURDER ON THE ORIENT EXPRESS

This is the tale of how an encounter with Jennifer Lawrence forced me to illegally record a coworker in order to avoid being murdered on the Orient Express.

Before I begin this murderous tale, I need to clarify something about myself. Until this story took place—I *swear on Ru-Paul*—I lived my life blissfully unaware that there were people in the world who did not like me. I'm not just talking about trolls on the internet who hate me for whatever I'm wearing or what my face looks like; I'm talking about the people in my day-to-day life, my coworkers, my friends. I didn't understand that some of these people could be legit talking absolute shit behind my back until I was in my mid-thirties. Sure, I assumed I wasn't everyone's slice of pie, but I've genuinely never had a female enemy or really been involved in any girl drama. (Keep in mind, I'm a real girl's girl: I grew up staring at other girls' bums in ballet class, was a professional dancer for two different entirely female NBA dance teams, and I kicked for Santa as a member of the Radio City Rockettes, one of the most famous female sisterhoods of all time.) Even when one of those girls went on to fuck my boyfriend, I would look at them and think, *well, they are gorgeous and charming, so I can kind of understand why.* I am simply not a woman who gets jealous of other women and then tries to tear them down. I am *that* much of a girl's girl. (And, if I do get that *totally normal* twinge of jealousy, I just use it as fire underneath my butt to work harder. I'm not perfect at this practice, but I've always believed that you have more to gain by working hard and being a stand-up human.)

Now, let's get into the story.

It was 2017 and one of the big Disney blockbusters of the year was *Murder on the Orient Express.* As a member of the press, I was to be flown out to Vienna to ride aboard the actual Orient Express (a jaunt that normally costs about $5,000 a night). We would soar through the Swiss Alps, snooze on the sleeper train, and wake up the next morning to interview the movie star Josh Gad in one of the famous train cars. The movie could've been just meh, and I *still* would've told the public it was the greatest thing I'd ever seen in my life because the trip was going to be so epic. I mean, whoever on the publicity team thought of this was genius!

I was so excited that I had been chosen to go! My travel

arrangements were already being put in place when I found out a small detail that sent a chill down my spine: The train cars would be two journalists per car, and I was set to be roomies with my first ever . . . *enemy*! Yep, I was pretty sure there was going to be a *real* murder on the Orient Express.

I don't quite remember how we became enemies because, again, I was at a point in my life where I was completely oblivious when people didn't like me. At the time, I was a young, hungry reporter on the fabled red carpet of Hollywood. Yes, my job was cutthroat—the top shows were always lined up neck and neck on the carpet, ready to scoop each other to get the "moment of the night"—but I prided myself on working with a collection of the most incredible girls I'd ever met. While we waited hours upon hours for stars like J.Lo to arrive, we would visit, and, eventually, we knew everything about one another's lives. I formed some adorable friendships. It was kind of like, *well, we're all in this together . . . even though at the end of the night one of us is going to be the clear winner.* However, there was one rotten egg of a reporter who seemed to stir up trouble wherever she went, *and* at the same time she always got the best headlines and was somewhat revered for her epic connections.

It's all really Jennifer Lawrence's fault. Enemy and I technically worked for the same company, and we shared a producing team and a corporate computer system. I had been sitting in an interview room and, because she was on the bigger show, she got to do her interview first. I had spent the week painstakingly going over and over my questions, making them unique and special because I knew I would be doing my interview in second position and didn't want any crossover or repeat questions with her. It caught me off guard when, one by one, Enemy asked every single one of my questions verbatim the way I had written them into the office computer program. I was livid! I don't think I'd ever been this standoffish or angry about anything in my life because I had no time to redo my questions. Before I even had a chance to understand what was happening, I was sitting in front of freaking Jennifer Lawrence and asking her *my* questions that were *word for word* the *exact* questions she had just. Been. Asked. *By someone else in the same room.* I was mortified. Chris Pratt came in next, and by the time it was time to interview Chris, whom I had formed a lovely sort of interviewer friendship with over the years, I was so distraught that I had tears in my eyes and stopped my interview to say, "I'm so sorry I'm a mess today." *On camera!* Needless to say, when the celebs left the room, I went wild. A lack of sleep, a super high stress level, and the fact that I had lived most of that year on the verge of a mental breakdown did not help. I tried to get Enemy to admit she had stolen my questions, but she denied it. From then on, it was war.

I would have panic attacks driving to work if I knew that our time in the makeup chair would cross. I had eleven eyes open at every single moment moving forward, and I was lucky that I did because I watched her successfully deceive everyone around us. The worst part was that no one seemed to notice. And, since karma is a bitch, over the next two years, I got a front-row seat to this person *winning.* Anyone who feels like someone may have wronged them knows that the absolute worst feeling in the entire world is when the person who has caused you pain . . . *wins.* Listen, I was used to being a loser and not being the shiny star of anything I had ever been involved in, so my frustration was less about *her* winning and more about when someone who is "not nice" rises to the top. She was crazy talented but had sunk so low in order to win: She lied all the time, she made things hard, she was mean to the people we worked with, and she was such a master manipulator that anytime anyone would complain or have her take responsibility she would gaslight everyone so expertly that all of our heads would spin.

So when I got the call from the producer that we were going to share a room together in the middle of the Alps covering a murder story, I knew I had to be the bigger person. My strategy was this: I would simply apologize for whatever my part had been in our misunderstanding about the interview questions and the rivalry that had followed. While I didn't feel like the bad guy, I was okay with taking one for the team if she could also admit that she'd also been kind of a jerk. After all, we were definitely pitted against each other in the industry, and it was an unfortunate series of events that had led to the strong emotions.

I put on my big girl panties and walked into the makeup room to speak with her. Here is the part of the story where I share my dirty little secret. I went into that face-to-face with a voice recorder in my pocket *without her knowing.* I was terrified of her spinning my words. I wanted to record the entire exchange to make sure I had proof if I somehow ended up in my bosses' office, *again.* However, Google tells me that, "Generally, it is illegal to secretly record oral communications between two or more people." So, really, I was being the shady one.

I started with explaining that I was sorry for my part in this. I told her she was talented, beautiful, and that I needed to say sorry. I told her everything. I was honest and vulnerable. In return, I expected her to put on her big girl panties, too, and perhaps offer her own apology for the damage she had done to me . . . but I had expected too much. She just sat there crying for thirty minutes, harping on her long list of horrible things I had done to her and why this was all my fault and that she was perfect. I asked if we could please move forward in a positive way, that we never had to like each other or be friends, but all of this back-and-forth war had to stop. We eventually came together to decide this was all my fault, that I was a horrible evil person, and that she had done nothing wrong, which was not at all what I thought was going to happen nor what I deserved, but oh well. We agreed to make a truce and I left.

I was emotionally exhausted and cried in my car the whole way home. When I got home I took off my big girl panties, took a hot fucking shower (and a Xanax), and went to bed praying the next day at work would be better. I was cautiously optimistic. But, I was still not looking forward to the closed quarters on the Orient Express. Having an enemy is so stressful!

Then, a glorious, glorious, *glorious* thing happened. Karma was served up on a beautiful platter for me . . . Enemy missed her flight to Venice and, in turn, would miss the train! My apology had been for nothing! I was going to live another day! I ended up on the trip solo, and it was the best three days of my life. I had the most fun ever with the fellow journalists, and at one point we were in the café car singing show tunes with Josh Gad and the rest of the cast at three in the morning. Epic.

I don't really remember speaking to Enemy ever again after that. Shortly after that roller coaster of the almost-murder, Enemy found herself on the losing side of the never-ending TV hamster-wheel of "you're in and you're out," and she was out. I lasted a few more years after her until it was my time to go, too. Years later I saw her wedding photos, and she looked freaking gorgeous and seemed really happy.

I spent many years in therapy thinking about this conflict and the trauma that these years working in an unhealthy environment did to me. My therapist likes to say to me that no human is all good *or* all bad, we are all good *and* we are all bad. I find that really comforting and now know that it's absolutely true. I know that whatever demons were eating Enemy alive during this time, she, like me, was both good and bad. But I also knew she was gaslighting me. She was making me feel like I was *all* bad and she was *all* good, and that simply wasn't the case.

I also learned a lot from being publicly despised at work. I truly believe that an apology is golden, and even if it's not your fault you should sometimes say you're sorry, too. My favorite personality trait is self-awareness. You may not be aware of what's happening in the heat of a passionate or upset moment, but it is important to be aware enough to know that the way you treat the little people is the way you treat the big people . . . is the way you treat the people you hate . . . is the way you treat the people you like.

I read once that you have to be okay with the fact that you might be the villain in someone else's story and, yes, I'm okay with that. I really am. But I'm also glad I didn't get murdered on the Orient Express. I still have the secret recording saved on my phone.

JAC: DEATH BY PENIS

A note to Mom and Dad: Please skip this story!

Now that we've gotten that out of the way, this is the fascinating tale of how I was almost killed by a penis. I'm not kidding. A dick almost murdered me. I swear to God this is a true story. Let me explain, but first a little bit of back story.

December of 2018 was a crazy time. We were smack dab in the middle of filming *LadyGang TV*. (For those of you who didn't get to watch the seventeen episodes of glorious garbage, LGTV was the . . . you guessed it . . . TV version of our podcast.) It was wild and crazy and a shit ton of fun! But, for me, it was infinitely exhausting and soul crushingly stressful. I felt like a literal fish out of water, and my anxiety almost always outweighed the thrill of this "once in a lifetime" opportunity.

A typical twelve-hour day of filming LGTV went a little bit like this:

5:00 a.m.: Wake up

5:30 a.m.–7:00 a.m.: Glam, chug a coffee, scarf a bagel down my mouth hole

7:00 a.m.: *Start drinking heavily* (because we were way funnier when we were drunk, duh)

7:10 a.m.–1:00 p.m.: Film the show

1:00 p.m.–2:00 p.m.: Lunch break (except we used this time to record our podcast instead . . . so no break for us)

2:00 p.m–5:00 p.m.: Individual interviews (think Bravo-style)

I also had a few fun personal issues that made being an overnight TV host exceptionally stressful. One, all the early morning drunkenness translated into me working all day with a continuous hangover. Two, I *never* slept the night before a shoot day because I was so anxious. And three, there was just *so* much pressure to be funny. I'm talking about a team of thirty production people and executives standing outside watching and judging every single word/comment/utterance! Listen, I never claimed to be a stand-up comedian! Nor was I a performer! I'm just a quirky emo kid who made graphic tees in college. I had never even been on TV before. . . . How the fuck did I get here?! The introvert in me was *not* made for this career, but I was thrust into it anyway and had to use every ounce in me to make it work. But that's a whole other story for another time and possibly my therapist!

Anyway! Now that you've got the back story, this tale begins with a full day of filming LGTV. I slept a whopping zero minutes the night before, so my whole day was fueled by the fear of disappointing everyone in the control room . . . and a full bottle of champagne. We'd film, I'd get drunk, we'd film more, I'd get hungover. Just a typical day in the office, right? Usually, when we were done filming, I would head home to scarf my face with McDonald's and watch *Arrested Development* until I passed out, but that day was different. That day was special. That day, we were jet-setting to the East Coast to appear as guests on *Today with Kathie Lee & Hoda*.

Drinking wine with Kathie Lee and Hoda was a *literal bucket list item*! Sleep was for the weak! I didn't even mind the stabbing migraine because I was so excited to jump on a red-eye to NYC to join our fav ladies in the a.m. Now, I usually despise red-eyes because I can't sleep on planes to save my life, but because we had our fancy TV show on E!, they paid for fancy first-class seats on the flight. Surely I could sleep on a fully reclining seat, right? (I even popped a Xanax for good measure.) *Wrong.* Just like the night before, I spent the entire flight wide awake and wired as shit, staring angrily at Becca and Keltie for six hours while they slept next to me like cute little babies.

We arrived in NYC at 6:00 a.m. and headed straight to the hotel to jump immediately into glam for the show. We were so tight on time that I didn't even have a minute to rinse off my disgusting airplane body, and I was dozing off while the makeup artist tried to glue eyelashes on my dried-out bloodshot eyes. But, you know what? It was all worth it. We spent a whole three minutes with Kathie Lee and Hoda, and it might have been the best 180 seconds of my life. While we didn't actually drink wine with them, I probably still had some wine in my system from the flight so I can technically check that one off the good ole bucket list. We even brought them a giant, human-sized wine glass as a thank-you present (which I'm sure went right into the trash, but whatevs)!

Afterward, I was on such a high from my epic morning that I forwent a (much needed) nap. My fiancé, Jared, flew into NYC for the momentous three-minute occasion, so of course we had to celebrate with a boozy li'l brunch . . . which turned into a dinner . . . which turned into a competitive game of late-night darts at one of my favorite bars on the Lower East Side. And before I knew it, I had been awake for sixty straight hours. And during those sixty hours, I had been drunk, hungover, sober, drunk, hungover, sober, and drunk again. Oh, and all of this was without *any* water. Oopsies.

Jared and I finally left the dive bar around 2:00 a.m. and headed back to our hotel. At this point in my life, I was still smoking weed to help me sleep, despite the fact that it almost exclusively sent me into an existential spiral every single time. (Like, my mind would immediately go to everyone I love dying and slowly floating off into the abyss like George Clooney does in the movie *Gravity*. I know, I know, so calming right?) So I busted out my weed pen, and Jared and I took turns puffing on what I now call the "Existential Nightmare Machine." I immediately went from tipsy to tipsy X buzzin', which is honestly just a euphemism for horny. Because nothing, and I mean *nothing*, is better than an orgasm when you're stoned.

Before I continue, let me sidebar here to remind you of the state of my body at this time: sixty-plus hours of no sleep, very little water, lots of coffee, and now high as shit. Dehydrated, drunk, stoned, jet-lagged, and straight up exhausted. #healthy-living babyyyyyy.

So Jared and I started fooling around in between taking drags of the ENM, and within minutes his face was in between my legs giving me the best oral I've had in my entire life. And that's when it started happening. The existential doom of being a little bit too high started slowly creeping into the corners of my brain. And then death. *So much death.* And then . . . I morphed into George Clooney, trapped in a claustrophobic astronaut suit slowly floating off into the nothingness of space.

And this is where it got weird. Because, as my mind was literally spinning into the depths of hell, my body was in the most intense state of euphoria I'd ever experienced. It was a literal detachment of mind and body. I was at a crossroads, so I decided to lean into it. I leaned into the orgasm. I leaned into George. *I'm the astronaut now.* And soon the existential panic dissipated, and the intense bliss took over. As my orgasm hit, my space suit burst open! And instead of sorrowfully floating into the void in that heavy-ass suit, I was speeding through the galaxy a million miles an hour, completely naked! Running my hands through the cosmos. My vagina literally bursting with shooting stars! It. Was. Awesome. And it didn't stop. That orgasm kept rolling and rolling and rolling as I was zooming through galaxies a million light years away.

During this never-ending orgasm, I brought my brain back down to reality enough to tell Jared I wanted to have sex. I barely finished the sentence before we started having the best sex of my life. We started doing a position I recently learned is called the "Viennese Oyster," where I was on my back, with my legs bent at the waist and my ankles behind my head. I was basically bent in half, but it is a great angle to hit all the right spots. So not only was I rolling through the most intense clit orgasm of my life, I started having a G-spot orgasm simultaneously. And then, as I was continuing to glide through the infinite universe in a blissed-out state, a black hole started approaching on the horizon. And before I knew it, it was starting to swallow me. And then BOOM.

Nothing.

And when I say nothing, I mean literally nothing. Everything just. . . . stopped. I couldn't see, I couldn't hear, I couldn't move. I was in the void. There was only darkness. And I stayed there for what felt like hours.

Did I die? Am I dead???

And as fast as everything disappeared, everything came crashing back into frame. I had fucking *fainted. In the middle of sex.* What felt like forever in the abyss was literally less than five seconds. When I came to, Jared was holding my shoulders, with a terrified look on his face, asking me if I was okay. Slowly, my senses started to come back. I blinked a few times trying to get my bearings. And then . . . panic.

And for anyone wondering what a panic attack might feel like after you fainted when you're way too high . . . 0/10. Would not recommend. The moments that followed were the most terrifying of my fucking life. I spent the next few hours thinking I was going to die while also wondering if I was already dead.

It all started with my heart pounding a million miles a minute. I thought I was having a heart attack for *hours* and kept begging Jared to take me to the emergency room. Then I started shaking. And then I couldn't stop shaking. My teeth started chattering. And my arms and legs started twitching. And then as my entire body was convulsing, I started having a literal out of body experience, which I recently learned is called "depersonalization." I floated to the top of the room and was overlooking Jared and myself sitting on the bed in this bizarre dreamlike state for what felt like hours. And then I just . . . lost all of my senses. I couldn't speak. I could barely see. I couldn't feel anything. I kept making Jared touch my arms and legs to see if I could feel it and it just felt like . . . nothing. It felt like his hands were just going straight through my body.

I spent the next few hours in the fetal position, making Jared basically put all of his body weight on me to stop the shaking and so that I could feel *something*. I eventually fell asleep in the wee hours of the morning and woke up feeling like I was hit by a truck (shocker). And the cherry on top was that we had to film an interview at 7:00 a.m. that morning after I semi-came back to life. You can search on YouTube for "LadyGang Build Series" and watch my brain shut off and buffer multiple times in the interview. I guess the exhaustion and dehydration and stress and drunken hangover and being too high and cutting off circulation to my brain wasn't a great combination for survival. Huh, who woulda thought? I still wonder if I did actually die that night and am now living in an alternate universe. I guess I'll never know!

In conclusion, the love of my life almost murdered me with his penis, which is equally horrifying and impressive. Bravo, Jared, *bravo*.

LADYGANG CONFESSIONS

NIP SIP

I was a tandem-nursing mama, which meant I breastfed both my young toddler and my infant at the same time. Not literally at the same time, but they were born close enough in age that I had not one, but two hungry babies to feed. To apparently everyone in the universe who is alarmed when they hear that (because you know, everyone loves to tell moms how to be better moms): Yes, my infant did get enough milk, and no, my toddler did not take it all. In fact, both of my babies were off the charts in their growth . . . which is where my problems really began.

Having hefty, healthy breastfed kiddos meant that my body produced milk. A *lot* of milk. Enough to feed a small army type amounts. Even with both of them feeding, I would have to use a Haakaa pump every now and then. So when I say I made a lot of milk, I really mean that my body was seemingly making new milk, constantly, in excess. When my toddler went to spend the weekend with my parents, this became a rather big issue. I was still making the milk that he would usually drink, but not as much milk was getting emptied from my breasts, since he was gone. This led to clogged milk ducts, which is a super common experience for nursing mothers.

I'd had numerous brushes with clogged ducts in the past, but this time, none of the usual remedies were working. Epsom salts? Nope. Vibrations? Not a budge. Hot water? Massage? Sunflower lecithin? Nursing and nursing and nursing in tons of different positions? Thoughts? Prayers? Curses? Forget about all of it.

Nothing was helping. It seemed like my pump wasn't strong enough to pull the blocked milk down, and neither was my little baby's sucking. Now, I'm a busty gal with two breastfeeding babies, so suffice it to say that my tits were hanging low and had about as much firmness as a bike tire that had been sitting untouched in the shed for two decades. Meaning—well—that my own nipples could fold right on up to my mouth. That's right, you

heard me: After all other methods failed, out of absolutely dire desperation, I went to work unclogging my own tits. Now, if you've ever had a clogged duct, you know that you will do any-thing, absolutely *anything*, to make the pain stop. It's truly hor-rible. The good news? It worked! I was the only thing around that was strong enough to unclog the duct. Sweet relief. The bad news? As it unclogged it shot out like a fire hose. Right into my own mouth. So yeah, I (accidentally) breastfed myself.

NATURE'S LUBE

Ahh, the dreaded yeast infection. Truly one of the worst things about having a vagina. Unpredictable, inconvenient, and always staying too long. Overall, extremely uncomfortable. I had just started dating my now-husband and got stuck with a nasty one. Itching and burning out of control—the whole nine yards. But of course, did I tell him? Never! I refused to ruin the honeymoon phase!

So, a few days later, when he wanted to go down on me, I let him. It was one of the best oral experiences of my life. Not because of the orgasm, but because his scratchy tongue felt so good down there. Kind of like a bear rubbing its back on a tree. Of course, with any yeast infection, in addition to the endless itching, there's always some other rather unpleasant side effects like the awful discharge situation. Well, I let my new boyfriend go down on me, and he kept exclaiming, "Oh my God like you're so wet you're so wet!" I was not wet with sexual oozes—I was wet with rotten vagina. It might not have been the finest moment, but a girl's gotta do what a girl's gotta do to get some relief before those antibiotics kick in.

GASTRIC LIE-PASS

After two kiddos and many years of a happy marriage, the only thing I wasn't happy about was my body. My husband never said a word, but it just really weighed on me—quite literally. Nothing I did seemed to help me drop any weight. Finally, tired of trying and failing all sorts of diets, cleanses, and exercise regimens, I flew to Mexico about four years ago and got gastric sleeve surgery. And I didn't tell a soul.

My husband of fourteen years doesn't know to this day. I did all the research, used my own cash, and cooked up a clever cover story to help explain the trip and the subsequent results. I told him I was flying to a chic wellness spa in Arizona. I pulled up resorts and showed him websites, discussed the treatments I was hoping to get, and even asked for his opinion on what lectures and activities I should pick. Of course, I was actually flying across the border to get a surgery to cut my stomach in half!

During my recovery I even called him a few times and gushed about how great I was feeling, how much I was loving the meditation, how I was feeling much more centered, yada yada yada. When I came home, I kissed my husband and kids hello and went on as if nothing had happened. Over the next few months, I lost around sixty-five pounds and was feeling really good.

My husband was amazed, having seen me struggle for years (and again, never saying anything about it—gem that he is). I told him it was all due to my new mindset and wellness.

I have some scars from the laparoscopic surgery, but they're so small he hasn't even noticed. The caesarean scars from my first babies probably helped cover that up. But then, get this— about two years after my surgery, I got pregnant with our third kiddo. I obviously told my physician about the surgery for safety, but the doctor made sure it was never brought up when my husband happened to attend a prenatal appointment with me. When I delivered my baby via C-section, the doctor even found a staple left over in my abdomen from my stomach surgery! I told my husband that was crazy, and that it must've been from a previous C-section, which he totally bought.

I don't know why I kept the truth from my husband, especially at this point. I think I was embarrassed that I had to resort to such a drastic measure to achieve my ideal weight. I didn't really want to have that discussion with him, worried he would think less of me. I don't know if I'll ever tell him. Now, the sweet man goes around telling people how incredible it is that my previous physician left a staple in my body for over ten years!

66

I am involved in a BDSM community where I participate in kinky activities similar to what is seen in *50 Shades of Grey* (but not sex), at a public dungeon. I like when people gather around to watch.

99

WHAT'S MY AGE AGAIN?

I met my now-husband when I was nineteen and he had just turned twenty-three. When we first met, he made a joke and called someone a "kid" who was twenty. I thought he was super hot, and was really just looking for a casual hookup, so I lied and I told him I was twenty-one. (Hey, my fake ID looked pretty good.) Well, the joke's on me because our casual hookup quickly became a long-term relationship. I was able to hide my real age by frequently "forgetting" my wallet at home and claiming that I "didn't like the taste of alcohol."

This lie got even worse when I met his parents for the first time a little while later, and they insisted on me having a glass of wine at dinner. His parents are pretty straight-laced, and I was still underage, but there we all were, at a table, drinking together. The other issue is that my husband has a sister who's one day younger than me—or at least, one day younger than my fake age. That means his whole family has no trouble keeping track of my fake birthday. At this point, he's still never seen a birth certificate, and it's been nearly a decade of none of them knowing how old I really am.

SOMEONE CALL NEV!

I've been using my own best friend's pictures to catfish a married guy I met online for the last four years. First of all, she has no idea about it. Although I've talked about meeting someone online, I never told her that it's her face all over my profile. I fully copied her entire photo feed, pretended it was me, and started up a conversation with this guy. As in, I totally faked what I looked like, thinking it couldn't possibly come back to bite me in the ass. Initially, it was just something fun—a way to distract myself. But then we started to get deeper and deeper, and I absolutely caught feelings. He lives across the world from me, so there's not really a chance of us just running in to each other, but we've been talking for so long that now I'm stuck in a hard place.

I'm madly in love with him, and he's madly in love with me. But the other factor is that I've been in a relationship—an actual IRL one—for the past two years. He wants to finally meet now, and it's killing me because I have no idea how to even go about breaking that kind of news to someone. Someone call Nev; this deserves its own episode!

I HAD SEX WITH SOMEONE IN THE BACKSEAT OF A CAR WHILE MY EX WAS IN THE FRONT SEAT. AND AFTERWARD, I WENT AND HAD SEX WITH MY EX, TOO.

TRIPLE SCOOP

I am #sorrynotsorry that I'm about to ruin your favorite ice cream duo, but this is one of those stories that's been begging to be told for too long. It was August 2017 and I was dating this guy who we'll call Ben. Now Ben was super sexy and mature. He was just plain fun. The type of guy you could have sex with multiple times a day and never get tired of seeing naked. Even though Ben and I were super casual, of course I was a little bit in love with him. One night, Ben and I went out to a club for some drinks and some fun. We were tearing it up on the dance floor and making out, and he had his hand up my skirt rubbing my clit. God it was good. Of course, five tequilas deep, I needed to take a pee break. When I returned from the bathroom, there was Ben, cozied up to his super-hot ex-girlfriend at the bar.

I was so mad, but I decided to play it cool. I went up to speak to him, but he pretended he didn't even know me. So, me being me, I left the bar and went to the one across the street where I ran into Ben's equally attractive best friend we'll call Jerry, who just happened to be standing outside. I got my flirt on in order to get back at Ben. The next thing I knew, best friend Jerry and I were making out in a cab on the way back to his house where we proceeded to have wild passionate sex. To date, it was the best ride I have ever taken. The man was a luxury full-sized vehicle. After an hour of pure revenge ecstasy, I got off my joyride and checked my phone. There was a huge, long text from Ben, confessing his love for me, and letting me know he wanted to be exclusive with me. The reason he was so cozied up to his ex was that he was telling her that they were done forever, and she wasn't taking it well.

I was in shock. I was also totally dehydrated after a night of booze and the ride of my life so I headed to the kitchen for some water and to clear my head a bit, and who is sitting on the couch but *Ben*. Yup, I had totally forgotten that Ben usually stayed at Jerry's after a night out when he wasn't at my house (because his place was forty-five mins away).

I quickly lied and told Ben that I'd come to Jerry's to surprise him, and that I felt the same way about him. He was so turned on, he threw me on the couch and started passionately making out with me. Shortly thereafter, Jerry came looking for me, fully naked, and to his surprise, what did he see? Ben and I, on his couch, just about ready to have sex. Jerry stood there confused for a few seconds, and then the next thing I knew I was bent over, Ben balls deep in me, while I sucked Jerry off. We ended up having the most passionate threesome ever. And that's not all. Our little trio continued for an entire month. We would get together three or four times a week and have absolutely incredible sex. Needless to say, August 2017 was the best month ever. While none of us stayed together, we still hang out in the same circle of friends, and I'm actually going to be a bridesmaid in Jerry's wedding. It's a secret only the three of us know, and, oh boy, do I get horny every time I'm in their company.

HE ATE THE BAIT

My now-husband and I met online. Very early in our relationship I knew he was the one, but he was dragging his feet on being in an exclusive relationship with me, saying he wasn't sure if he was ready. That annoyed me, so I decided to teach him that I was a better option than playing the field. He was still on the dating app so I created a fake profile and catfished him. Made a date with him and everything, and then he went to meet "her" for the date, and nobody showed up. Afterward, he sent the fake profile a message saying, "wow, what gives," and I never responded. Shortly after that, we became exclusive. Two years later we are randomly talking and he tells me about this girl he met online who stood him up, and it was then that he knew he was done with dating. I've never told him that it was me, and never will.

NO REGRETS

I had an abortion when I was married. I told my husband it was a miscarriage, but really, I knew he was someone I could never have kids with and our marriage wasn't working. I didn't want to bring a kid into a shit situation. We are divorced now and I don't regret my decision. I know we really had no business getting married—a ring, a dress, and a big party don't fix anything.

LEARNING THE BREASTSTROKE

I have been sleeping with my kid's swim instructor—who is twelve and a half years younger than me—since June. It's been the hottest, most exciting, anxiety-inducing, gut-wrenching, give-me-more-I-can't-quit-you "relationship" I've had in my life.

This is what happens when you fall head over heels in lust with someone: You realize you are willing to do ridiculous things to avoid being caught and to keep the whole thing going. Things like learning to "accidentally" trip the breaker so my security cameras will stop working, or how we use the downstairs bedroom (which is my parents' room when they come out to visit for the winter). Or how I was with him until 1:00 a.m. the night before I had to entertain sixty-plus people for a birthday party the next day. I could go on and on, but basically, I have completely lost my head and am loving every minute of it.

It all started when I developed an innocent little crush (or so

I thought) on my kid's swim instructor at her swim school. Well, as time went on, he really started to get under my skin—he's just so good looking. I found myself imagining some very inappropriate situations, and not just when we were at swim class. After having kids, I felt like a shell of the cooler and sexier woman I once was, and something about this man woke me up inside. I was hot and bothered!

Of course, I couldn't stop thinking about him. As the warmer months approached, I developed my plan to get him to come and do lessons at my house. We exchanged numbers one day. I began my quest by just talking about business: swim lessons only. Which, of course, morphed into friendly texts that eventually turned into long chats about life.

When I found out how much younger he was than me, I made a flirty joke alluding to the fact that I was old enough to be his mom. To that, he replied that if he ever saw me out, he would show me what "this son could do." Awful, I know . . . but I was *so* there for it. The messages became more inappropriate from there, then turned to photos, until eventually things became physical. And that was the beginning of the hottest fling I've ever had.

It's definitely not a relationship—we'll go days or weeks without talking, but somehow, we always end up back at it.

Needless to say, while he may have taught my kid how to swim all summer, he's taught me a few things as well.

"

My husband thinks I'm getting in shape for summer, but I'm really getting into shape to leave him. Most people lose weight and get fit *after* a divorce—I'm getting fit so that when I do divorce him, I'll be hot as hell doing it.

"

A UNIQUE ARRANGEMENT

A few months ago I was sitting around with some girlfriends, and we got on the subject of push presents and mommy bonuses. Some women in the group had experience with a push present— basically just some extravagant gift a man gives a woman after she's given birth. I've heard of women getting jewelry, a trip, a purse, and sometimes a set amount of money deposited in their bank account. Mommy bonuses are sort of similar. At the end of the year, if the husband works and the wife doesn't, when he gets his bonus, he calculates one for her, too. There was this big stink about it in the news a few years back because someone wrote an article about the women of the Upper East Side of Manhattan getting hundreds of thousands of dollars for managing the household, keeping themselves toned, and getting the kids into the right schools.

My girlfriends were pretty split on the idea of financial compensation for motherhood. I kind of stayed silent—because, while my husband and I don't partake in a bonus structure, per se, we do have a sort of . . . unique arrangement.

My husband and I both work full time. We split all the household bills and babysitter costs, but otherwise keep our money in separate accounts. We've always been pretty independent about it, and it works for us. Since he technically makes a lot more than me, he has more extra money sitting around in his savings than I do. He's a typical guy so he doesn't enjoy shopping much, and never seems to need more shoes, or jewelry, or purses. But what woman doesn't want a little more money sitting around? As we've gotten older though, this has presented an interesting solution to avoid any particular conflict in our marriage.

In my mind, our sex life is great. I consider us very sexually satisfied—but my husband's sex drive and desire to "try new things" is constant. He always seems to want it more and in more interesting ways than I do. So, as a way of balancing the scales a bit, I have, on more than one occasion, allowed him to pay me several hundred dollars to try something new that I was just not as keen on trying. For example, he really wanted to try anal, and I was a bit on the fence about it. We talked it over, settled on an amount, and one deposit later we were off to the bedroom. I am not ashamed to admit I have absolutely zero guilt about it. I have extra cash in my savings and a spicier sex life, and both of us are happy. I now do most things anyways, but it was kinda fun and even made things sexier. I would do it again in a heartbeat!

ONCE HAD A GUY GO DOWN ON ME IN A PANTRY. A LITERAL "SNACK."

CHILDLESS WONDER

I'm a twenty-seven-year-old gal who has known for my entire life that I didn't want to be a mother. I don't like kids, and I don't feel the need to have one just because everyone expects me to. This has been an issue in past relationships, so I told my current boyfriend that I physically can't have kids so he doesn't think I'm just a heartless bitch.

100% THAT SNITCH

I have this male friend. I've known him for years and he's great, but his personal life tends to be a mess. Usually his escapades lean more toward funny than potentially disastrous, but one day, he told me he was having an affair with a girl he used to go to high school with. She was married with kids. For some reason this really bothered me, and I just couldn't laugh it off. It was also the latest in a series of ever-escalating personal life disasters for him, and it seemed like someone needed to teach him a lesson. So I did what any upstanding citizen would do and sent a message to the woman's husband through a fake Facebook profile. I told him she was having an affair and that he should probably take a peek at the private messages on her phone. I had never met the husband nor the wife, so they had no idea who I was, and the Facebook page I started had no picture and a fake name. He never responded, but I could see that he'd read the message.

About a week later, this friend came by to catch up over a few beers. I casually asked him how things were going with the married lady, and he told me that the husband had called him and told him to never see his wife again or he would beat his ass. My friend never found out that it was me. I think he learned his lesson—to this day, he's never had an affair with a married woman again.

I CLOCK INTO WORK EVERY MORNING ON MY PHONE WHILE STILL IN BED AND GO BACK TO SLEEP ¯_(ツ)_/¯.

SHAG 'N' BRAG

I went on a trip to London with my sister and her family. I was essentially there to be the babysitter. However, I was alone most of the trip because my nephew ended up getting really sick, so I just traipsed around the city by myself, which was actually pretty fun. I felt bad because they were all stuck back at the hotel, but I wasn't going to waste a golden opportunity to explore. I mean, it's London!

One evening, I decided to go to a bar. I honestly don't remember how I found this place, or what possessed me to go inside, but once I did, it was like I'd stumbled into a film set. Literally every man in this bar was gorgeous. Every. Single. Man. We are talking about handsome, gorgeous hair, gorgeous suits, gorgeous bodies, and shockingly gorgeous smiles (and those accents). I sat down at the bar and pulled out my phone, doing that thing where you sort of pretend to be busy while scoping out the merchandise. An absolutely glorious man who was a dead ringer for Jude Law in *The Holiday* (that might be a stretch, but not much), sat next to me, put his hand over my phone, and said, "We don't do that here." I fibbed a little and told him I was waiting for a friend, just to keep the conversation going. With his impeccable manners, he offered to buy me a shot while I waited for her. As the night went on, it became clear that my nonexistent friend was never going to show—which was just fine with us. We had more shots and danced a ton. He asked if I wanted to go back to his place . . . I did.

Of course, it turned into a whole night. We ended up having sex on essentially every surface of his apartment. We finished in the shower, in what was probably the most sensual experience of my life. When I say it was like something out of a movie, it was. His amazing flat, his sexy moves, the sort of perfect coincidence of it all. Truly one of those out of body experiences. By the end of this magical evening, my phone had died, and I had no idea where the fuck I was. Being a perfect gentleman, he got me a taxi back to my hotel and even came with me to make sure I got there safely. I never saw, heard, nor spoke to him again, and no one, especially my sister, knows where I went or what I did that night. To be honest, I don't even remember his name, but that kind of makes it even more perfect, in a way. The ultimate one-night stand.

I once got my ass eaten in the
Panda Express parking lot.
LOL.

DOC AND DASH

I spent a solid afternoon at HomeGoods, as one does, shopping my little heart out. My cart was full, and as I was checking out, I totally forgot to put a picture frame up to be scanned. As I was unloading it all into the car, I realized I didn't pay for the frame. The line was so long I didn't want to go back in for just the one frame, so I left without paying. Kind of like accidental petty theft. I know it's sort of like, "who fucking cares," but I felt bad about it, because, you know, *stealing*, so obviously, I told my mom.

My mom decides now is the absolute perfect time to tell me a story that I'd never heard before. When she was a young twenty-something, she was a flight attendant. Living it up, always on the go. I've heard a few cool stories over the years, nothing too crazy, but it always sounded pretty glamorous. Apparently, it wasn't fun all the time, though. Once, she was in another state (away from her home base) and her appendix burst. She was rushed to the hospital and needed immediate emergency surgery. This was more than forty years ago, so times were different, and when she went in, she gave them only her name—they didn't have any other info about her yet. When she woke up in recovery, the first thing she thought was that they would be coming to get her insurance information.

At the time, she didn't have insurance and was pretty broke, so she had no idea how she was going to pay for the procedure. Every time the nurse would come around she pretended to be sleeping. Finally, after successfully avoiding her for another round, as soon as she could move, my mom picked up all her stuff, got dressed, and just left. Straight up walked out of the hospital, got back to work, and flew home, states away.

Weeks go by and she thinks she just might have gotten away with it, until one day, my grandmother gets a call from the hospital across the country. They're asking for my mom by name, but my grandma, being the absolute G that she is, said, "I'm sorry, I don't know anyone by that name," and *hung up*. That's right—she just hung up the phone on the poor hospital administrator tasked with hunting down the runaway flight attendant who ran out on her hospital bill.

To this day, my mom never paid for her appendix surgery, and she was never found out. She made me promise not to tell anyone, but it's too funny not to share with the LadyGang. Needless to say, I definitely feel a lot less bad about stealing the stupid picture frame.

MY DAD CHEATED ON MY MOM AFTER THIRTY-PLUS YEARS OF MARRIAGE. THE NEW GIRLFRIEND LEFT HER BELONGINGS AT MY FATHER'S HOME. I SAW HER LIP GLOSS AND HAD NO CHOICE—I SHOVED IT UP MY ASSHOLE AND PUT IT RIGHT BACK IN THE TUBE. LITERALLY, KISS MY ASS.

SUPERCALIFRAGILISTICEXPIALI-FELON

I used to be a nanny for a very, very rich family. Like private jet rich. Like, Forbes 100–level rich. It was all kinds of crazy. I'd signed up for it thinking it would be cool to travel the world, get paid to watch a cute kid, and live in ridiculous places for free. While it definitely had some perks, overall, it was like living on another planet. This was the type of family that had multiples of everything. Multiple houses, multiple cars, multiple problems, and pretty much zero awareness. What I saw in those houses convinced me that as your net worth goes up, your net sanity goes way down. Thankfully, the parents weren't a total horror show like some of the stories I've heard, but they were pretty checked out. They tended to be careless with their things and would leave really expensive or one-of-a-kind items just strewn about. They would get frustrated if something took too long, or felt even the slightest bit inconvenient. It was sort of like they had forgotten what living in the real world was like, since they could just pay someone to do everything. Once, the mom left a stack of $100 bills for us so we could order sushi when they went out to an event, which led to a super awkward encounter at the door when the poor delivery guy couldn't break them.

Speaking of $100 bills, as the nanny, they gave me the code to one of their safes in case of emergency. (That's right—*one* of their safes—there were multiple, and some of them were comically, cartoonishly large.) I never really thought twice about it until one long weekend when I was watching their kid for a few days. During naptime, I started to poke around, just to see what I could find. Out of curiosity, I cracked open the safe. Inside were stacks. And stacks. And stacks. Of more $100 bills. Absolutely piles of cash. It felt like I'd stumbled into a scene from *Narcos*. It was like the entire GDP of a small country—just crazy.

Over the next few months that I worked for them before going back to college, I would just waltz on over to that safe and take a few $100 bills off the top of the piles and save them for a rainy day. I'm not at all proud . . . but they never even noticed the money was missing. At first I worried there might be some sort of alert every time the safe was opened, but no one ever said a thing. I know it's bad, but they paid me a minimum hourly wage and were so rich they literally didn't even notice when a few Benjamins disappeared. All right, it was more than a few, but I was a broke college student. I know it's terrible, but damn, that cash bought me some incredible clothes. No regrets.

REVENGE IS A DISH BEST SERVED BBQ'D

I grew up in this tiny town in Canada. It was the sort of place where everyone knew everyone, and people tended to settle down. If you met a nice guy and you hadn't seen him before, it was like hitting the jackpot. At eighteen, I was ready to get out because I was tired of the same old slim pickings. One evening, I was out at a bar and started chatting with this guy. I hadn't seen him around, so that was reason enough to strike up a conversation, but we hit it off. We chatted late into the evening, and he invited me to his friend's place the next day for a backyard hangout. He was super cute and flirty at the bar, and I was young, so I immediately figured there must be something there. By the time I showed up to his friend's place the next day, I had already imagined our entire future life together.

I took one of my good friends with me, and we showed up to this house that was essentially a frat. The house was gross, the yard was gross, the guys were pretty gross. None of them were very nice, and they ignored us for the most part. They kept going on and on about this barbecue they had just purchased. I guess each of them chipped in $50, so they were all standing around with beers admiring it. They were not the best company to be around. What's worse, the guy who invited me ended up being an absolute douche. Total one-eighty from his flirty, sweet behavior at the bar the night before. He was totally blowing me off whenever I tried to say something to him, flirting with my friend instead. I'd had a few too many drinks, and I ended up crying, which led to my friend and I getting into a bit of a fight with these guys. She tried to tell him off for his bad behavior, and he just shrugged us off. So, we left—decided to have some girl time, and let them all get back to staring at that stupid barbecue.

Later that night, my friend and I were a bit wasted, walking around town, trading stories back and forth about how ridiculous and shitty men could be. We wanted to think of some way to get them back for the terrible time we'd had and the horrible behavior of Bar Boy, and we just couldn't stop laughing about how obsessed they were with their barbecue. As we got closer to their house, my friend got this devious look on her face and said, "You know what, I have a shit cramp. I'm going to take one for the team." We found a box in the alley; she squatted down and did her business, and off we went. We snuck back into their yard, opened the lid, and poured that box of poo logs straight onto the grill of their brand-new prized barbecue. We ran off cackling into the night feeling like Thelma and Louise. Absolutely disgusting, but also absolutely iconic.

THERE'S NO "I" IN THEFT

This is a *full* circle story so keep with me. In high school I was on the cross-country team. We'd have to practice every day after school, running miles and miles and miles around our town. We would get pretty bored running for so long, so we decided to give our other teammates challenges. We started out with silly things, like running through someone's yard, or making them run the full practice in a silly outfit. It was pretty harmless.

Of course, as the season went on, we escalated things a bit and ended up with what we thought was a hilarious tradition: We used to collect lawn gnomes from people's front yards. Seriously. Every single gnome we could find, we'd nab it and run off. The uglier, weirder, and bigger the better. That became a mini challenge in and of itself. We'd snatch the gnomes and put them in a spot in the woods we called "Gnome Land." There were like a hundred of these little suckers just hanging out there by the time people caught on. I guess the people in our town, which was pretty little, finally realized all their garden gnomes were missing, and they called the police. (Like I said, it's a small town, so I guess things were kinda slow.) They did some digging around, and the next thing we knew Gnome Land was raided. Every single one of the gnomes was confiscated. We were weirdly bummed about it, but we moved on.

Flash forward to senior year, and I was at a house party that got busted. As they lined us all up outside to take down our names, I got arrested for an unpaid parking violation I was unaware of (like I said, our town didn't see a lot of police action). Low and behold, I was taken into custody. While that still feels a tad dramatic for a parking ticket (and my parents were definitely far from thrilled,) it was so worth it for what I saw when I got there.

As we pulled into the garage of the police station, I looked to my right and there they were! The shelf of *all* the confiscated lawn gnomes. Every single one, just sitting in this garage, looking out over the squad cars. I absolutely lost it. I was cracking up, and the police officers who were with me had no idea why. They asked me if I knew anything about the gnomes, but I didn't snitch. The next Monday, we made the front-page newspaper for the party. The townspeople were pissed, but our entire cross-country team was never busted for Gnome Land. I'm honestly still 100% glad I got arrested that night.

"

I licked one of
those Himalayan
salt lamps in
HomeGoods
because I
wondered if
it was salty.
It was.

"

YOU'S A HOE-GIE

I've always laughed extra at Becca's story about peeing in another girl's purse, because that was equally low to my secret! I was dating my high school sweetheart, and we were very in love. Total puppy love: mooning over each other all the time and weirdly protective of each other. I'd get jealous if I thought even for a second he was looking at another girl. I'm sure it was absolutely obnoxious to be around, but we were young.

I worked at a Subway at the time that was pretty much run by the teenagers who worked there. We spent our shifts having sex on the prep table and smoking weed in the freezer. The place was constantly buzzing with staff and friends of staff on the sandwich line. If our friends came in and wanted to hang, great. If it was quiet, we'd just chill. If it was busy, we would often throw a Subway shirt to them and have them come behind the counter so they could hang with us without getting into too much trouble. Total animal house.

My boyfriend was always there. One day, someone invited some girl I'd never seen before to come by and handed her a standard-issue Subway button-down shirt. She spent the rest of the shift totally ignoring the guy who'd brought her and flirting with *my* boyfriend. Totally immature stuff—acting extra sexy and annoying while she pretended to make sandwiches, that sort of thing. She put the shirt on with nothing underneath and only buttoned one single button in between her boobs. She was driving me nuts, but I was too quiet, shy, and sweet to say anything to her face. As if the one time wasn't enough, she kept coming back. Day after day, trying to make moves on *my* man! When my anger reached a boiling point after a few too many hours of this,

I decided to send her a message: I recorded a song from a CD to a cassette tape (yep, you read that right!) and wrapped it up. It had a bow and note with her name on it, and I think I even drew a little heart. I carefully placed the gift on her car just before I knew she'd come out, and hid to make sure she got it. When she saw it, she looked super excited and quickly got into her car. I imagined how happy she probably was, pulling off the ribbon, putting the tape in and hitting play, thinking it was a love song from a secret admirer. I couldn't really see her reaction as she drove away, but I still can't help smiling knowing she was about to hear Ludacris tell that boyfriend-mooning bitch, "you's a hooooe, you's a hooooooe!" I never told a soul, but, damn, for the rest of that shift I felt like a million bucks!

I USED TO WORK AT A DEPARTMENT STORE AND I WOULD PUT CLEARANCE STICKERS ON FULL-PRICED ITEMS AND BUY THEM WITH MY DISCOUNT. NOT TOTALLY STEALING BUT STILL PROBABLY STEALING.

CHARLES IN CHARGE

When I was in high school, my friend (we'll call him Matt) and I found one of those little key-chain credit cards they used to make in the early 2000s. There were all these articles predicting that they'd be the next big thing. Everyone was going on and on about how convenient it was to just have your keys with these mini key-chain cards rather than having to grab your whole wallet—but let me tell you: What was most convenient for us was when we found one of those little suckers on the ground.

The first name on the card was Charles. I'll leave out the last name because I'm still scared after all these years. Like the little burgeoning felons we were, we cut a slot for it in another card and glued it in place so it could swipe, but no one who saw us use it would question the name on the card. I have no idea how we figured out how to do this in the pre-YouTube era, but we managed to make it work, and we were pretty impressed with ourselves.

We used it for an entire summer to get gas. We did multiple road trips that year, and at least three of us were using it regularly. It was the best summer ever. We were absolutely living it up—music festivals, trashy bowling alleys, the closest beach, the local 7-Eleven parking lot (high school students are so lame)— Charles took us wherever we wanted to go! It was great. None of our friends could figure out how we were living so large, since we all had the same sorts of crappy, low-paying summer jobs, but we kept it a secret.

At some point Matt and I got scared we were going to get caught, because we'd been at it for a few months. As much fun as we'd had on Charles's dime, we were pretty sure our tab was running itself up. That was also when gas stations started putting up cameras, so we figured it was probably better to abandon our new life of crime before it caught up with us. On the last trip we took with Charles, we made sure to top up our tanks, and then we chopped him up. We threw him out the window at various places on our drive home, and that was that. That summer was sponsored by Charles, but it was over and we were back at school, being poor again. To this day, I wonder how rich that guy was that he didn't notice all those charges. Did he just not care? Was he just not paying attention? Did the bank forget to cancel the card after he reported it stolen? I think about it a lot. At the same time, it was 2003, and my little Honda needed only about $10 to fill the whole tank, so maybe we weren't running that bill up quite as high as we thought!

A LADY ALWAYS TELLS

t's now time for you, our reader, to think about your own deepest, darkest secrets. What are you holding on to that you need to let go of?

LadyGang is *clearly* not a trio of scientists, but this little experiment of ours has made us think about the damage we do to ourselves by keeping all of this embarrassing, regretful, cringy energy every day. So many of us have this hidden shame floating around our brains with no way to let it out without being judged, and that shit weighs us down. We drive ourselves crazy worrying about what everyone else is thinking about us, without realizing that everyone around you is probably preoccupied with their *own* shit weighing *them* down. So, what we've learned is that one mistake or action doesn't define us as a person. Everyone fucks up every single day, and we all need to give ourselves a little bit of grace. Sure, we can be judgy bitches sometimes, but we need to collectively chill out a bit. Sitting on your high horse and being the Mistake Police doesn't help people *not* make mistakes; it just teaches them to be more secretive when they *do* mess up. And so the unending cycle of feeling self-conscious about our lives continues. Not to get too fridge-magnet on you, but we all really need to focus on making better mistakes tomorrow.

Whether your secrets are mortifying, heartbreaking, full of cringe, or just mistakes you'd never make again, we need to let go of the idea that we should somehow be embarrassed about our lives. We hold on so tightly to the things we don't want anyone to know, and yet somewhere some man is literally getting high fives for announcing he's cheating on his wife to a bar full of strangers. We are committed to leaving shame and guilt in the past and moving forward owning our secrets, laughing at our stupidity, and learning some important lessons along the way.

The not-so-secret realization we've learned is that none of us is either all good or all bad. Let that sink in for a moment. You, reading this right now, *you* have been the good guy and the bad guy endless times in your life. You have been the antagonist in at least one person's life story. You have been super-duper lovely, but you have also been a jerk. You've waited until your group is called to board a plane, but you've yelled at the flight attendant when she cut you off from your fifth chardonnay. You've helped an old lady cross the street, but you've stolen from the tip jar. You're the best romantic partner on the planet, but sometimes you flirt with your high school boyfriend on Facebook just for fun. You've held your best friend's hair while she puked from too much tequila, but you've called her a drunk behind her back. You've lied to get what you want, and you've been livid when someone lied to you. Being a human is complex and nuanced, and we are living in the ever-changing moral gray area. Good and evil live within all of us all the time, and *you* are the only one who decides where you fall on the spectrum. As long as you didn't hurt someone physically, emotionally, or mentally, stop feeling bad about the gray areas of your life that have made it exciting and uniquely *yours*.

So, whether this book has inspired you to tell your best friend your deepest and darkest, or to tell your therapist the 100% truth instead of the 80% truth, congrats! You are a little bit lighter than you were yesterday. After reading this book, we hope that, if nothing else, you feel a little better about your own imperfect self. Sex is messy. Motherhood is impossible. Relationships are tricky. Bodies are weird. We are all struggling in one way or another. But if we've learned *anything* writing this book, we've learned that stumbling through life is a lot easier when you have your ladies by your side.

And lastly, we had so much fun writing this book that we are keeping the secrets hotline open! If you are inspired to share your secret with us, please visit theladygangsecrets.com or call 1-844-SXY-LADY. We will be sharing our favorites on upcoming episodes of our podcast, *LADYGANG*.

ACKNOWLEDGMENTS

Thank you to our wonderful LG community for embracing their own Ladysecrets and being brave enough to share them with us. We personally read and listened to every single submission, and it was a daunting task to decide what should be included in this book. Your humor, honesty, and vulnerability was our good week, each week.

Thanks to Diana Baroni, Danielle Curtis, Tammy Blake, Christina Foxley, and everyone at Rodale. Wesley Bird for your incredible talent and illustrations. Andy McNichol, Sara Shapiro, Carolyn Conrad, Sue Madore, bleeping-out-the-fucks expert Jared Monaco, our Podcast One and LivexLive team: Kit Gray, Sue McNamara, Sam Brosnahan, and Steve Delameter. Our Be-Social team Haley Henning and Ali Grant. The incredible Kat Nejat-Thompson, Matthew Busch, Claire Leahy, Chelsea Parker, and Taylor Rondestvedt for all your hard work. Alexandra Ingber for being our best-kept ladysecret. A huge thanks to all our friends and family for the support when to the outside world it looked like we were "crushing," but to our inner circle we were having kelt-downs. Jeri, Zach, and Chris—we love you. And to baby Ford, thanks for being our best-kept secret, and welcome to the gang.

ABOUT THE AUTHORS

The LadyGang began with a podcast with the mission to make women feel less alone. Since 2015, the show has boasted over 175 million downloads, topped the podcast charts, and spawned a television series, clothing line, accessories line, and book. *LadyGang* the podcast was a People's Choice Award nominee and a Webby Award nominee for best series, has been featured on *Entertainment Weekly's* coveted "Must List," and was judged "Podcast of the Year" in 2016. The creators—Keltie Knight, Becca Tobin, and Jac Vanek—have appeared on *Good Morning America, Today,* and *Entertainment Tonight,* and have been featured in *People, Variety, Who What Wear, The New York Times,* and *The Hollywood Reporter.* Their first book, *Act Like a Lady,* was a *New York Times* instant bestseller, a *USA Today* bestseller, an Amazon best pick of the month, and a *Toronto Star* bestseller.

Also by *New York Times* bestselling authors
Keltie Knight, Becca Tobin, and Jac Vanek

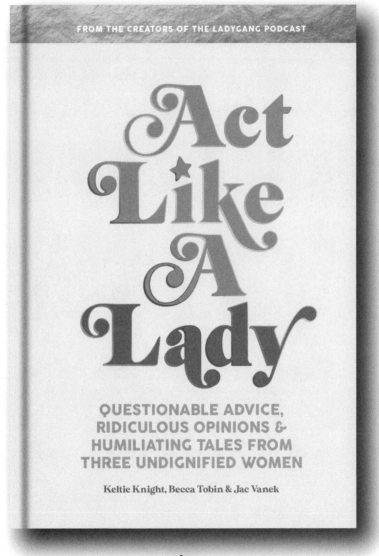

FROM THE CREATORS OF THE LADYGANG PODCAST

Act
Like
A
Lady

QUESTIONABLE ADVICE,
RIDICULOUS OPINIONS &
HUMILIATING TALES FROM
THREE UNDIGNIFIED WOMEN

Keltie Knight, Becca Tobin & Jac Vanek

RODALE
BOOKS

Available wherever books are sold